# "I KNEW YOU'D COME!"

## Stories from a firefighter

## By
## Colin Ive

Published by Colin Ive

Copyright ©2006 Colin Ive
colin.ive@smecontinuity.com

Cover design by Elliot Wilsher, Calvary Design Ltd
www.calvarydesign.com

Printed by the Friary Press, Bridport Road, Dorchester

ISBN 0-9554593-0-3
ISBN 978-0-9554593-0-6

For my wife Brenda and children Jenny, Stuart and Robert who had to put up with their husband and father doing what he did. Without their support it would have been impossible.

Acknowledgements
My thanks to John & Margaret Mills and Cathy Howard for their time, encouragement and suggestions on reviewing the manuscript.

# Contents

# Introduction

I will never forget the last fire I attended; we put out a blazing gorse bush in an area of Yateley where we had extinguished blazing gorse bushes many times in my 25 years as a firefighter. I vividly remember my first fire. It was as a member of a very green crew sent to the aftermath of a serious house fire in Hawley. We needed to gain experience after months of seemingly endless training.

The years between were filled with a richness of experiences covering the range of human emotions. More positive than negative with a few really weird ones! This book captures a few of these experiences. It records some of the incidents that my fellow firefighters and I went through at Yateley. These stories are not about statistics, target levels or league tables, they are about people. They are about the firefighters and a few of the many people we came into contact with during these years of serving our community.

We dealt with fires, floods, rescues, road traffic accidents, air crashes and a famous medieval castle fire. Importantly we also contributed to the safety of our community with simple advice and programs including the importance of having a working smoke alarm and wearing a seat belt. Finally we were pleased to be able to raise many thousands of pounds for both local and national charities.

We laughed thousands of times and cried a few. None of us will ever forget our years as Yateley Firefighters.

# Foreword

The stories in this book are taken from personal experiences gained during the twenty five years I served as a Yateley firefighter with Hampshire Fire & Rescue Services. Twenty three were as the first officer in charge of Yateley Fire Station. I have made great effort to accurately share the events and emotions I experienced over that time. Though others will have seen things from a different perspective, these stories are as accurate as my memory, coupled with research, allows.

To help the reader understand some of the terms or 'jargon' we use in the fire service I have included the following.

## Acronyms

FF = Firefighter

LFF = Leading Firefighter

RTA = Road Traffic Accident

HFB = Hampshire Fire Brigade

HFRS = Hampshire Fire & Rescue Service

> In 1992 Hampshire Fire Brigade changed its name to Hampshire Fire & Rescue Service to better reflect the service it provided.

BA = Breathing Apparatus

AFA = Automatic Fire Alarm

AFS = Auxiliary Fire Service

NFS = National Fire Service

## Explanations

Fire Ground – The area within which a fire station is responsible for the first attendance following a 999 call.

Branch – The nozzle which fits on the end of a fire fighting hose.

Hose reel – A high pressure fire fighting hose pulled off of a rotating drum.

Jet – A length or lengths of joined low pressure hose with branch attached rolled out and joined by hand.
Pump – The mechanical device used to push water through the hose. Can and is also used as a term to describe a fire engine. i.e. 4 pumps equal 4 fire engines.
Fire Engine – A noisy big red thing with flashing blue lights!

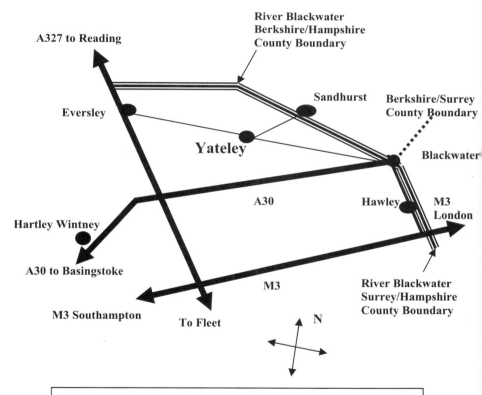

Map of Yateley Fire Station Fire Ground.
Bounded by the M3, A327 and River Blackwater

# Chapter 1

## Windsor Castle Fire

The vast majority of the calls we responded to we had little prior knowledge of what to expect before our pagers went off. This was not the case however with probably the most famous incident we attended.

At around midday on Friday 20th November 1992 Berkshire Fire Brigade received a call to a fire in the Queen's private chapel in Windsor Castle. Upon their arrival they found a significant fire developing in the Brunswick Tower, a part of the building dating from medieval times.

Although looking at a castle it appears to consist mainly of stone its interior has considerable quantities of timber used for floors and walls. These timbers are often very old, extremely dry, and have been modified and added to many times over its long history. The result of such work over many years for Windsor Castle in 1992 was an external stone structure supporting numerous internal wooden corridors, rooms and panelled walls. These also had the added feature of numerous voids behind the panelling. The consequence of so much timber and voids upon the fire was to allow it to travel between rooms and corridors with some ease taking full advantage of the timber fuel it found as it progressed.

It was the flames which resulted from this process that not only lit up the sky in Windsor but whose images were broadcast and lit up the news bulletins of hundreds of television news channels being beamed into millions of homes around the world.

Amongst this global audience the Yateley fire fighters were also watching. Well most of them. Being located so close to the Berkshire border we took a particular interest in it for as the fire grew so also grew the number of fire fighters required to fight it. Located only 20 miles

8

from Windsor we anticipated a call, and were not disappointed, though initially it was not to Windsor.

At 18:24 hrs we responded to our pagers and arrived at the station to find we had been sent to stand by at Bracknell fire station. Such moving around of fire engines is common when a large incident requiring multiple pumps occurs. As areas become devoid of their normal fire cover so pumps from surrounding areas are spread around to maintain the best possible service to the community.

Standby duty can be filled with the tedium of hanging around on a station waiting for a call which never comes and as a result this was not the most popular of calls for busy retained firefighters with family commitments to spend their time on. Nevertheless although not the call we anticipated a crew was quickly assembled and we made our way to Bracknell.

It may be noted at this point that although most of us were aware of the major fire in progress LFF John Hicks was not. Seeing that the call was just to stand by John decided not to come along because he had a family commitment that evening and stood down to let another firefighter take his place. It was only later when watching the evening news that John realised he had missed out on "The Big One". An action which was commented upon right through to his retirement. Not that this diminished in anyway the colossal contribution that John made to the station.

Arriving at Bracknell we found the fire station was busy as that evening a social event had been planned for which some firefighters' wives were still preparing food in readiness. Due to this major incident the event was eventually cancelled. We helped out by being more than happy to help eat this food whilst watching the still large fire at Windsor being broadcast live now on 24 hour news channels. We were however becoming more and more frustrated at not getting the call we all hoped for. The night wore on and some of use tried to get some sleep. Then in the early hours of the morning the call finally came and we joined the firefighters from 12 different county fire brigades at the scene.

By the time we arrived the fire so vividly seen devouring the contents of the Brunswick Tower area of the castle had been knocked down. But there was still considerable smoke issuing and significant challenges still to be overcome. Not the least of these was the problem of trying to isolate the fire and so stop it spreading throughout the remainder of the building. Axes were taken to the ancient timber walls and floors to create fire breaks and though in the main this was highly successful significant pockets of fire still remained.

We commenced our operations, along with other crews, in the Chester Tower. Although comparatively undamaged this tower was under direct threat from the fire spreading to it via the castle flooring.

It was around this time that representatives of the world's media were allowed to enter the grounds and were placed upon the grass around the central keep from where they could film and broadcast. It became somewhat embarrassing for seniors officers who had informed the media that the fire was under control when a significant column of smoke started to develop from under the Chester Tower. It was only after some frantic hard work by the firefighters present that this threat was extinguished and further red faces avoided. It was during this time that we made a notable rescue, Prince Andrew's golf bag containing clubs and balls, the latter of which we were disappointed not to find marked with his personal monogram. However this did not stop us from reciting in future years of the day we rescued Prince Andrew's balls!

We all worked hard that morning, with some being rewarded with a breakfast in the royal kitchens. It was a truly remarkable scene to see the royal lawns covered in fire hose, fire engines and firefighters. Hundreds of firefighters attended from nine county brigades and hundreds more were involved in the continual moving of appliances in order to maintain fire and rescue cover over a vast area of central southern England. But after a considerable amount of hard work the fire was eventually extinguished and it was a tired crew who eventually returned to Yateley at 11:55 hrs, 17½ hours after the initial call and the longest spell on continual duty we ever experienced.

A few weeks later the following letter arrived from Prince Charles personally thanking us for our work.

*Dear Mr Ive,*

*Having witnessed the terrible scene of devastation at Windsor Castle last Friday and having met some of the people involved in tackling the fire, I wanted to write to express my profound admiration for the superbly professional way in which the firefighting teams carried out their dangerous and difficult task.*

*So often we seem to take for granted the crucially important role played by the Fire Service and other emergency and rescue organisations, but I fully appreciate the degree of organisation, planning and training which is required to produce the type of response we witnessed last week. The very least I can do, therefore, is to ask you to pass on my heartfelt congratulations to all the members of your team for the calm and courageous way in which they dealt with this particular disaster. I am convinced that had it not been for the rapid and effective measures taken by the Fire Services to deal with such a complex conflagration the damage to the Castle would have been infinitely worse.*

*We all owe you and your colleagues a great debt of gratitude and I hope you will convey my best wishes to those involved and, in particular, to those who received any injuries during the operation.*

*Yours sincerely*
*Charles*

In addition I was pleased to meet the Prince at a reception he gave for retained firefighters from across the British Isles. When I was introduced to him he was informed that I had attended the castle fire and I began to sympathise with him about it. But he smiled and said "Come off it, you lot like nothing better than a bloody good blaze!" I could only agree with him.

Our ability to attend and successfully participate in the fire fighting at Windsor Castle was dependent upon numerous factors spreading back over many years. The stories of just how these factors all came together follow.

# Chapter 2

## Yateley has it own Fire Station – At last!

In December 1966, the Yateley Ratepayers and Residents Association made their first bid in a campaign to have a fire station built in Yateley due to the rapidly growing community. An extensive review of the fire cover for the area was conducted resulting in the Chief Fire Officer of Hampshire reporting that there was nothing, at that time, to justify altering the existing arrangements for the area. There was however, recognition given to the likelihood of continued growth in the area and that the situation would have to be monitored.

During the 1970's the area of Yateley and its neighbouring village of Blackwater became the fastest growing area in the UK as substantially more and more housing estates were built and people moved out of South and West London in search of the lower cost housing the area had to offer. At the same time the completion of the M3 motorway made travel so much easier in the tri-county areas of South West Surrey, South Berkshire and North Hampshire.

As the population continued to grow so came with it an increase in fires and incidents requiring the services of the fire brigade. In Yateley several significant house fires occurred during the seventies, including one which gave me my first taste of the devastation fire can wreak.

Sleeping peacefully in the early hours of a hot summer's morning in 1976 my slumber was shattered by piercing terrified screams. Stumbling out of bed I threw back the curtains. Through the window I could see flames and smoke pouring from the windows of a neighbour's house. Falling down the stairs in my rush and almost without thinking I ran out the front door and across the road before clearing, though I don't remember doing so, a five foot high wire fence.

Suddenly there I was below the hysterical mother with smoke billowing around her at the upstairs window. She threw out her first baby to my waiting arms as another neighbour joined me in time to catch a second child.

The mother then swung herself down from the window ledge and fell onto us. Finally the father, a large round man, appeared and without hesitation jumped over our heads onto the ground behind us breaking both ankles on impact!

Looking up the flames now roared out from the window where the family had stood. The fire had become so intense that the father had burns on his feet as they made their escape.

During the period from the closure of the World War II fire stations, see Appendix at rear of book, and the opening of Yateley Fire Station in 1982 the fire cover for the area was provided by Hartley Wintney, Crowthorne and Camberley Fire Stations.

Many residents saw this as no longer adequate to meet the needs of the newly developed area. Eventually following continued demands, and (it was thought by many) the biggest fire in memory when the parish church of St Peters was burnt down by an arsonist, Hampshire County Council agreed in 1979 that a fire station would be built and staffed by retained firefighters.

There are two kinds of firefighter. A wholetime firefighter is located on busy fire stations and attends there for 42 hours a week on a shift pattern basis. During this time they train, eat, rest and sleep on the station ready for calls. A retained firefighter is located on a station with just a few hundred calls a year, often a great deal less, and lives close by. They have a fulltime job in some other capacity, and dedicate many hours a week to be available to respond and attend emergency incidents.

Often, if able to respond from their normal place of work, this availability can exceed 150 hours per week. They are alerted to an emergency by the pagers they carry. Emergencies which could, and often did, occur at the most inconvenient time and interrupt all types of human functions. Alerted by their pagers they drop everything and respond within a few minutes to the fire station. Here instructions on the location and type of incident await them on a teleprinter.

Retained firefighters are the first line of fire and rescue response for their community and are qualified in fire and rescue duties, after a great deal of training, to the same level as their wholetime colleagues. Although seldom realised by the general public retained firefighters solely staff over 60% of all fire stations in the British Isles which in turn represents 95% of its land mass. They also jointly staff, with their wholetime colleagues, pumps at a great many other stations.

In early 1980 recruitment began in Yateley. Advertisements and a recruitment caravan were set up in the shopping area of the town where more information was supplied and people were encouraged to apply. Following acceptance of the initial application, interviews were then held at Fleet fire station. It was at these interviews that I first met Danny Randall. He would become a good friend and subsequently my right hand man for many years before succeeding me as the Officer in Charge.

All of those selected had their own motives for applying. My own journey to the recruitment door began several years before when visiting Mildenhall fire station in Suffolk. My wife, Brenda, had family in Mildenhall and three of her uncles were retained firefighters there. Theirs was a lively busy station. I was intrigued by the characters I met. On hearing their pagers they underwent a transformation from relaxed family men to focused dedicated professionals.

With encouragement from Brenda, I applied and was fortunate enough to be selected. One of 15 men who met for the first time on August 3rd 1980 to begin their long training and become qualified firefighters. Once this was achieved we were to be based at the then yet to be built Yateley Fire Station, located to the rear of The Royal Oak public house in Reading Road, Yateley.

During two long years of training we learnt about use of equipment. How to fight fires and perform rescues from a range of scenarios, though most notably focused upon the extraction techniques for cutting victims from car crashes, or Road Traffic Accidents (RTA's) as we quickly learned to call them. A selection of us passed the HGV qualification to drive the fire engine. Most of these men then went on to the advanced training enabling them to drive 'under blue lights.' That is to drive to an incident with blue lights flashing and sirens wailing. In addition they undertook extra training in pump operation. At an incident the driver takes responsibility for delivering the water to the hose.

All of us became qualified Breathing Apparatus (BA) wearers following an intense and personally demanding course in the stifling heat and smoke filled rooms and rat runs (pipes with a diameter of just over a shoulders width, or so it seemed) which all had to be successfully negotiated in order to pass. We learned there as much about ourselves as we did about the equipment and techniques for its use.

During our training time we learnt a great deal about working as a team in all the tasks we undertook. All of those who made it successfully through these years of training owe a personal debt of gratitude to Alan Albury. He was a wholetime firefighter of Sub Officer rank. He taught us so much, not just from text books but from his own personal experiences of many years as a firefighter. He ensured we were good enough to satisfy the inspections and drills by senior officers but also the demands and expectations of our community. Then finally the station was built and became operational, "On the run", in August of 1982.

In the first 25 years of operations these firefighters and those who followed responded to over 7000 emergency calls, ranging from serious fires both within the community and outside, notably the most famous being the Windsor Castle fire, to performing rescues and special services at aircraft incidents, RTA's, floods, chemical spills etc, etc.

A total of 43 firefighters have been fortunate enough to serve their local community in this way during these 25 years. I say fortunate because for the majority of these years there was a long waiting list of applicants eager to join. But once qualified a firefighter would often serve for many years and so recruitment as a necessity was low. Such waiting lists are rare on many retained stations where an acute shortage of staff is common. There is little doubt in my mind that the reason for the waiting list we had at Yateley was the high profile we continually gave the station. We promoted it regularly via local and on occasions national media so that our community knew who we were and never forgot we existed.

The station is a community facility and provides a community service, one that the firefighters have been dedicated to providing and one I believe those following will continue to provide.

This was not the first Yateley Fire Station and in an Appendix at the rear of this book I have given a short history of the Auxiliary Fire Service fire stations at Yateley and Hawley which were set up and crewed by local volunteers to protect their communities during World War II.

Before I relate further stories please see the following report and comment of a fire which took place in Cricket Hill, Yateley in 1904. It has been copied from the June 1904 edition of the Yateley Parish Magazine and held as a reference by the Yateley Society. It is the earliest record of a fire occurring in Yateley that I have been able to find and reflects well even then the demand by the local population for improvements in their fire fighting protection. A demand that after many years and a considerable increase in the population resulted in the opening of Yateley Fire Station.

### Fire at Bourne's Lodge

*The fire at Sir A. Godley's lodge, which resulted in the destruction of the house but happily without further loss, again calls aloud to the Yateley Parish Council to provide the parish with a fire hose. If such a hose had been in existence and there had been a hydrant on the main which passes the house probably the fire would have been got under control before serious damage had been done. We should like to ask the Parish Council how many fires they require before they wake up to the necessity of purchasing a fire hose. If they would only spend £5 a year in hose they would have a good length in four or five years, probably quite enough to cope with any fire they may be called to deal with. At present however there are no hydrants on the Cricket Hill main and their first cure should be to have them fixed. Perhaps it is not generally known that the Insurance Companies are always willing to reduce their premiums if there is a fire brigade and sufficient hose. The Churchwardens of Yateley got a considerable reduction when they bought 50 yards of hose for the use of the church.*

This extract from the Yateley Parish Magazine was taken from an archived edition recovered after the fire which destroyed St Peter's Church. The salvaged pages of the magazine were photographed as part of the work of the Yateley Society. Ironically these pages show clear signs of suffering serious fire damage.

# Chapter 3

## Gaining experience

The principles of fire. A simple method of understanding how fire exists, and how to put it out, is called the triangle of fire. The triangle consists of three elements, Fuel, Oxygen and Ignition, with these in place a fire will occur, by removing just one of these so a fire will be extinguished.

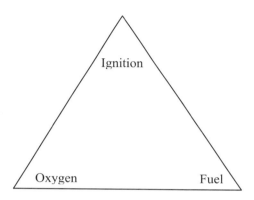

The Triangle of Fire

The most common way of fire fighting is to remove the ignition element by cooling the flames with water. This also has a smothering affect and removes the oxygen element. A better example of this latter affect can be found when a fire blanket is used to smother a fire. An important factor is not to remove the blanket until the fuel on fire has had its temperature lowered to below its ignition point or the fire, for example in a chip pan, will simply reignite.

When possible a simple way of extinguishing a fire is by removing the third element, its fuel. Creating fire breaks is a good example of this, a method often used in fighting forest fires. The fire becomes starved of the timber and undergrowth it has been consuming, progresses no further because of the break created between it and any further fuel supply and so extinguishes itself.

As firefighters most fires we dealt with we treated by cooling with water. Occasionally we arrived at an incident where the fire had burnt itself out by consuming all of the fuel available to it. Finally on rare occasions we would come across one which had extinguished itself by using up all of the oxygen in a room, or rooms of a building. Such cases can be extremely dangerous for firefighters if found when the room is still very hot and the material, or fuel within it is still above its ignition point. Should an unwary firefighter open a door or window so allowing oxygen to flood into the room there is the risk of a backdraught resulting in an explosion of fire, often with fatal consequences for the hapless firefighter. In 1996 two retained firefighters in South Wales were caught in just such an explosion with tragic results.

Firefighters Kevin Lane age 32 and Stephen Griffin age 42 of Blaina, South Wales, died in February 1996 dealing with a severe house fire. As a BA team they had entered and rescued a 5 year old child from the two storey building. Taking the child outside they were told that a second child was unaccounted for and thought to be still trapped inside. Kevin and Stephen did not hesitate and re-entered the blaze to continue with the search. In an upstairs bedroom they were caught in a delayed backdraught and succumbed to the severe burns they received. The second child was later found to have already escaped and been taken in by neighbours. Such sacrifices should never be forgotten.

Fortunately these incidents are rare but one of the most bizarre fire calls we attended took place one morning when called to a house fire. Upon arrival we found that incredibly it had put itself out by burning up all of the oxygen in the room of its origin. No windows or doors were open so no fresh oxygen could enter and it had snuffed itself out.

Investigations revealed that the fire had occurred during the previous night and only in the morning had a neighbour smelt burning and called us out.

On entry we found the cold remains of a smallish fire in the living room but one which had generated a great deal of toxic smoke severely contaminating the area. Sadly it was within this room that we found the bodies of a cat and dog lying dead on the floor. Upon removing their bodies and opening up the windows and doors to dispel the remainder of the smoke we were confronted with a bizarre sight. The carpet of the room had been white, although by now was covered in black soot, except from where we had removed the animals. There in front of us were their perfect silhouettes both in apparent full stride with the dog directly behind and so seemingly chasing the cat!

We made certain these shapes were obliterated before the owners and their children returned. Indeed whenever dealing with dead animals we tried to make the owners ordeal as light as possible by removing the bodies of their beloved pets.

**Domestic Garage Fires**

Domestic garage fires can be the most dangerous of incidents. Garages are invariably store rooms for all sorts of combustibles and explosives! These come in a variety of forms such as tins of paint, multiple aerosols, acids, chemicals, petrol etc.

Amongst the most dangerous calls of this type we attended was when we arrived to find a garage well alight and the lady of the house in great distress. Immediately we leapt into action and commenced rolling out hose in order to get water as quickly as possible on to the flames and knock them down.

I tried to reassure the lady and to find out whether or not anyone was in the garage. Eventually she calmed down enough to blurt out that what she was really worried about were the shotgun cartridges and black powder her husband had stored in there! It is at times like these that firefighters move their fastest. Which we all did directly away from the inferno finding cover where we could. Often it seemed at the time behind each other. With the area evacuated and jets of water poured onto the blaze from behind convenient brick walls it was eventually extinguished.

I recall two other significant domestic garage fires, due mainly to the naivety of the youths involved.

The first was caused by a simple and understandable mistake. Well it was if you were a bored fifteen year old lad. This young man and a few friends decided on a pleasant summer afternoon to have a barbeque in his back garden. Mum and Dad were out but he knew what to do, he'd seen his dad do it loads of times! Out came the charcoal and lighter fuel, a quick match and the 'barbie' was soon well alight.

Then, so disappointingly for the lads, the flames went out! Must be 'duff' charcoal they thought. Bored with waiting they cleared up, carefully tipping the charcoal back into its paper sack and returned it to the garage, an integral garage, of a detached house. Then off they went seeking new adventures.

A short while later a neighbour, seeing smoke pouring from around the garage door, realised that something was wrong and dialled 999.

This call was also memorable for us as we had just, and only just, extracted the pump from the mud we had bogged ourselves down into as we dealt with an undergrowth fire on Yateley Common.

We arrived before too much damage was done to the property but for a while it proved difficult to establish the cause. Then the young man returned home and sheepishly described what he had done. The charcoal had not 'gone out' but only ceased to generate flame and, as charcoal does continued to burn, it soon made short work of the paper sack and was duly working on the contents of the garage as we arrived.

The second incident of this nature was sparked off rather differently. This time the young man concerned was using his father's garage, again integral to the house, to work on a car he was rebuilding placing various vehicle components into trays of 'thinners', a chemical degreasing agent, situated under the bench he was working at, in order to clean them.

He was hammering out some metal, and for a while no problem occurred. That was until a spark from this hammering dropped into the fumes of the highly inflammable thinners. Then there was a big problem as these fumes exploded and the lad was extremely lucky to escape shocked but otherwise unhurt from the resulting fireball.

We arrived to be confronted with an intense fire. We quickly knocked this down but the garage was destroyed. There was severe smoke damage to the rest of the house which in turn resulted in many weeks of the family having to live in temporary accommodation whilst all was repaired.

I am pleased to report that both lads learned from their close shaves. Indeed despite on both occasions we heard them repeating over and over a common mantra of "My dad's gonna kill me! My dad's gonna kill me" they survived.

**A Spiritual Experience**

As the years went by and our experience grew, many of the calls became routine but then occasionally something unusual would occur. The strangest most thought provoking of such incidents was without doubt experienced whilst we dealt with a rare, though unfortunately not rare enough, fire in a post box.

Post box fires were often caused by a firework being dropped into the box. We dealt with them by emptying into it the contents of a dry powder extinguisher. Then after contacting the post office we awaited the arrival of a postman with a key to open the door to enable him to remove its contents. Prior to him completing this task we would inspect the ashes to ensure there were no remaining embers which could later develop into a major conflagration in a mail room.

This was the procedure we were following one dark evening in the early nineties. As we did so we were joined by Mike a local resident who I knew, along with the rest of his family, as members of the congregation of St Peter's Church. We chatted and he was very disappointed about the fire as he had recently written and posted a letter to his wife Ann. Ann was at this time undertaking voluntary work in appalling conditions at a run down orphanage in Romania not long after the fall of the Iron Curtain. A strongly Christian family Mike's letters helped to sustain Ann whilst working in this harrowing environment and they were greatly anticipated and treasured. I commiserated with him on the situation while waiting for the arrival of the postman.

It is a common feature of such incidents that when the box is opened all that remains of the letters it contained is a pile of ash, but not on this occasion. It did not look this way to begin with for as the door of the box was unlocked and swung open so a pile of ash appeared, some of which tumbled out as it did so. I carefully put my hand into the pile to check on any heat within it. As I did I immediately felt the paper of an envelope. Withdrawing it from the ash we were all amazed to find it had not a single singe upon it! I turned the letter over in my hand, but already I think I knew whose name would be on it. Sure enough Mike confirmed that it was indeed his letter. It should never have survived the fire but it did and was duly delivered and appreciated.

**The Mystery of The Burning Feathers**

The last story had a spiritual connotation to it but the following, though it took a while to work out, had a purely scientific solution.

The information provided for us on our teleprinter readout of a "boiler explosion" certainly had us expecting a far more serious incident than we found on our arrival. It was just how the incident had occurred at all which concerned and confused us for some time before eventually establishing its cause.

We arrived at the scene and found everything was peaceful with no signs of smoke, flame or destruction caused by an exploding boiler. Instead we met the lady of the house who was totally bewildered at what had happened but very aware that something <u>had</u> happened!

The scene of the incident was in the kitchen. There was little to see and what there was just seemed to add to the confusion. It was not a very large room and equipped with standard kitchen fittings of cupboards and sink unit. A gas boiler stood alone against the wall opposite the sink. There had certainly been a fire as one could still smell the smoke. Propped up against a wall in a corner of the room was the remains of a heavily singed feather duster. But no other obvious signs of burning. The only clue offered by the boiler was that the cover was lying on the kitchen floor. Though several feet away from the burnt feather duster. It was all very confusing. What had set fire to the feathers?

The first thing to do was to talk to the lady. She confirmed the room was unoccupied at the time she heard what she described as a bang. On entering the kitchen she found the room as I described but with more smoke in it which had dispersed prior to our arrival. Opening the door the cat had run out quickly past her. She explained that the cat came and went in and out of the kitchen via the cat flap in the back door of the house, but, she went on to say, she had only recently seen the cat in the rear garden and was surprised to find it in the kitchen.

The smoke in the air appeared to be coming off the feather duster, but it was faint and the smell it gave off was the worse thing. All very interesting but not a lot of help, or so we thought.

We then commenced a methodical search of the kitchen, including the cupboards and their contents. It was when doing this we had our breakthrough. One of the crew could hear a very faint hissing sound when he put his head into the cupboard under the sink. Removing the contents of the cupboard one item at a time we isolated this sound to the aerosol can of a well known kitchen cleaner. This can was quietly hissing away and escaping from it was the aerosol propellant gas. This was the clue we needed and the following solution to the fire was pieced together.

The aerosol can was quite old and being kept under the sink was frequently in a damp atmosphere, leading in turn to the rusting of the can. Rusting which became so bad that it led to the leakage of the propellant gas, a gas which incidentally is a) highly flammable and b) heavier than air. The gas seeped out of the can and forming a low laying cloud crept out of the cupboard and spread across the floor. All that was required was for it to come into contact with a naked flame and bang! A naked flame such as the one burning as the pilot light on the boiler! It would though need a disturbance of the cloud for this to happen. Enter the cat! As the cat came into the room from the garden via its cat flap so it created enough disturbance to fan the gas onto the flame and the resultant bang was then able to take place. The feather duster? The feathers were in the gas cloud, when this ignited it flashed over and lit the only available fuel to it, the feathers! Then having no other fuel to ignite once burnt simply went out, leaving behind just a haze of smoke and smell as witnesses to it ever happening in the first place.

**The Big Old House**

Firefighters always enjoy a situation most when one of their own has suffered some embarrassment or indignity. Interestingly there have been a fair number of these over the years. It would be wrong of me to tell too many tales of others without relating one which befell me, much to the amusement of the rest of the crew!

We had been called to a fire in a large Victorian property in the nearby village of Eversley. As we arrived in the road outside we could see smoke issuing from the ground floor and the driver did not hesitate for a moment in driving through the pillared gateway and positioning the appliance on the gravel outside the building.

After a brief assessment I found we were confronted with a small though intense fire in one of the ground floor rooms. I despatched two BA wearers using a hose reel to set about extinguishing this helped by the crew of a second fire engine who had just arrived from our neighbouring station in Hartley Wintney.

During my assessment I had discovered that the old house had been split up in parts into a series of flats and it seemed clear that not everyone had evacuated the premises. The smoke from the fire made anyone who was still inside the building a potential casualty. It was at this point that Station Officer Mick Robinson arrived.

Mick and I set about banging on doors to alert and evacuate anyone still there. From some of the flats we could get no answer and so had to force the doors open. One particular door proved more difficult to force than the others. We persevered and it finally sprang open. Both of us tumbled through the doorway straight into a bedroom. This action awoke the occupant who had until then continued to sleep blissfully on unaware of the shouting and banging taking place around him. His startled reaction was to leap up in the bed with fists raised prepared to take on these violent intruders. We soon calmed him down and, grabbing him a coat to cover his embarrassment, helped him out of the property. I'm still not certain though who was the most startled, him by our forced entry or us by this very erect figure of aggression bouncing up and down on the bed stark naked with fists raised!

Returning downstairs we found the fire had been extinguished. Although one of the BA wearers, FF Danny Randall, did admit that this task could have been performed a few seconds sooner had he not been trying to fight the flames he saw on the left of the room as he entered! Flames which it transpired were actually reflections in a mirror of the real fire located to the right of the room! A learning point we have mentioned many times over the years.

With the fire now out we then set about the tasks of ventilating the rest of the house to get rid of the smoke and make sure that the fire was not smouldering in the old wooden floor of the room. Before we did so I spoke with the elderly lady owner to understand more of the layout of the property. Being one of those who had evacuated the house she returned and informed me that below the room was an old cellar, though it was shut up and had not been used for many years. I thanked her for this information which I commenced to verify to ensure that the fire had not spread below the floor and into the cellar.

The house was dark and musty containing lots of dimly lit corners with cobwebs everywhere emphasised by the smoke particles now clinging to them! The old lady continued to insist that no one had been down to the cellar for years but agreed we could do what we needed to do.

She led me to the dark hallway where she insisted the only entry lay. There I pulled back an old musty rug revealing a trap door set into the floor giving access to the darkened unlit cellar. It was a large heavy wooden trapdoor with an iron ring used to pull it open. So it was on hands and knees I heaved and strained and the trap door at first reluctantly, slowly but surely creaked opened. It was noticeable at this point how quiet those in the room had become. They too waited to find out what was below. I peered in.

It was shortly after this that I was heard to exclaim loudly, some even said I screamed, and leapt back in fright as a beam of light stabbed out of the inky blackness below! Adjusting my now damp trousers I heard the familiar voices of the crew from Hartley Wintney, they had found another entrance to the cellar from outside and were merrily conducting their own inspection.

As I have said firefighters greatly enjoy another firefighters embarrassment and this occasion gave many of those present much amusement, and as old stories are retold has regularly done so for many years.

Once assured that there was no longer any threat from the fire we packed up our kit and began to make our way back to the station. There was though one last hurdle to negotiate. On our arrival we had driven the appliance straight through the gateway. Upon our departure we realised there was only about a one inch space either side of the vehicle and we had to carefully manoeuvre to get through. Entering the driver had expertly negotiated it perfectly first time.

Mentioning Danny Randall wearing BA brings to mind another call of our very early days. We had been called to a house fire and upon arrival were confronted with smoke pouring from a doorway.

Danny and FF Mark West, who was physically considerably the larger of the two, donned BA and grabbing a hose reel quickly made an entry through the door. Danny was leading but much to the annoyance of Mark he stopped.

Frustrated at not getting beyond the threshold Mark verbally and physically encouraged Danny to push on further. Propelling him forward proved somewhat uncomfortable for Danny as the door way was actually an entry into a simple cupboard measuring about 3 foot square. There was little enough room for Danny let alone the large frame of Mark. Fortunately Mark realised they were going nowhere fast and peeling Danny off of the not so far wall extinguished the rubbish fire on the floor of the cupboard.

**Going to the Dogs.**

From time to time it's necessary for a crew, often searching for a reported fire, to split up, some covering an area on foot whilst others drive the pump to a prearranged meeting point, making full use of the hand held radios to stay in constant contact with each other. Such instant communication offers significant benefits; that is until the strange sense of humour that firefighters suffer from occasionally takes over. Such an occasion is yet another very clear memory for me.

It was early spring. As a result of a dry period of weather our calls to grass and undergrowth fires had increased. On one particular evening we found ourselves on the third call of the day being directed by our HF&RS fire control to deal with an incident in a remote area to the west of Yateley common.

On arrival we could find no trace of a fire. Double-checking with our fire control we confirmed we were in the correct area. Darkness was falling rapidly and it was important to use the remaining light to find the fire or risk it flaring up in the middle of the night and the subsequent risk that this would pose to a nearby large conifer plantation.

The location we were at and the address given for the incident certainly seemed to correlate. But as we had learned from experience a given location can sometimes cover a much larger area than we may anticipate. I split the crew up and sent them out to comb the surrounding gorse and bracken. But search as they did this proved fruitless as still no sign of any fire was to be found.

This particular piece of common backed on to the grounds of a large house. This house had a swimming pool which we had used to good effect in a previous year when dealing with a nearby large common fire in particularly hot weather. (We used the water for fire fighting as well!)

Frustrated at finding nothing despite our searches I decided as a final check to walk through the grounds of the property ensuring that nothing was brewing within them. I sent the pump off to pick up the rest of the crew instructing it to meet me at the front of the premises.

So I commenced my walk. I soon satisfied myself that all was well at the rear of the house. Then I made my way along a garden path to an area alongside the main building. All was quiet and calm until I was within a few yards of the house at which point a crescendo of barking suddenly erupted. I saw to my horror racing out of the evening gloom towards me two very large Pincer Doberman dogs extremely well endowed in the dentistry department and obviously intent upon fulfilling their guarding duties to the maximum!

Fortunately I knew exactly what to do in this situation and making full use of the fear welling up inside I stood stock still as though petrified, not a difficult state to achieve at that moment. This, or so I thought, seemed to stop these hounds from hell in their tracks for although still exercising their canine vocal cords to their fullest they came no closer.

Clearly my situation appeared precarious. I felt that if I moved they would be sure to attack. But I couldn't stand there all night! It was then I thought of my friends on the fire engine. They'd be sure to help. It seemed easy for though standing still I held a radio in my trembling hand and by simply pushing the transmit button and talking quietly into it I could explain my situation and they would rush to my rescue. Well that is what I hoped!

Carefully and quietly I made contact and described my dilemma to them. The dogs by now had calmed and stopped their barking. But still paced the ground menacingly, growling repeatedly as they did so. There was a pause as I waited for a reassuring reply. But when it came it was not what I had in mind for over the radio, and into the still night air around me, came the sound of woofing and barking from my so called mates. Sure enough this had the immediate and desired, by them, effect of setting the dogs off once more and rekindling my worst fears.

This second round of barking had a more positive effect as lights in the prior to this darkened house came on and a man appeared calling the wretched beasts to him.

The man came over to me and viewed the quivering wreck of a firefighter stood stock still in front of him. The dogs were still in the open watching me carefully. He asked what was going on. I explained the whole situation whilst still nervously eyeing the dogs that seemed in turn to be continuing to lick their lips. Fortunately he quickly understood and went on to explain that I was in no danger as the dogs were fitted with a device which reacted to a cable laid out in front of where I was standing. In simple terms this delivered them a small electric shock if they attempted to cross it.

Now with the lights on and my eyes fully open I could see both the device around their necks and the cable. Indeed he said had I danced up and down with a string of sausages they would still not have passed the cable. I decided not offer to explore this theory any further but politely asked him to shut the animals away whilst I completed my journey and search. By now the original object of my walk had left my head and all I wanted to do was to get to the safety of the pump and my hands upon my good friends who resided within it!

No fire was found and no further incidents were reported over the next few days which could have originated from anything we had missed. I was satisfied we had taken the right action. I could even, as I share the same somewhat strange, some may say warped, sense of humour as my colleagues after a while see the funny side of the whole thing. But this did not sway me from taking any opportunity to reap my revenge!

**There's Off and There's OFF!**

Firefighters Mickey Barton and Chris Parker had never suffered from a personal hygiene problem. So the night their colleagues moved quickly away from them holding their noses, gagging and gasping for fresh air naturally came as something of a shock for them.

It all started with a call to a house fire on a local housing estate well known to us for minor arson incidents, usually involving cars or rubbish.

Upon our arrival at the incident a fire could be seen burning in the front room of an apparently empty house. I immediately despatched a BA team of two firefighters, Mickey and Chris, to deal with this and conduct a search of the premises. Gaining entry via the front door this team soon found that the fire was in an old armchair which they quickly extinguished.

Breathing apparatus is an essential part of a firefighters protective equipment. It enables them to survive and work in heavily smoke logged buildings ensuring a continuous supply of clean air in their face masks at a higher and so positive pressure to that of the normal atmospheric conditions around them. This positive pressure ensures no smoke, fumes or toxic gases affects the firefighter, although it also negates their sense of smell of everything outside of their mask.

As I waited in my customary position of crouching below the escaping smoke by the front door and entry point of the BA team. I started to detect an odd unpleasant smell emitting from somewhere inside the property. The smell became so bad that I moved away from the doorway and made my way along the building to the adjacent front room window of the house, seeking to establish the progress of the team. Meanwhile Mickey and Chris had made good progress. With the fire extinguished they undertook a thorough search of the entire house opening windows as they went to vent off the heavy smoke logging.

About this time others outside of the property began to notice the increasingly obnoxious odour.

The BA team worked on and became satisfied that the property was empty and contained little in the way of furniture. Although they later mentioned that they did notice that there seemed to be a 'squashy' and sometimes slippery substance underfoot. Undeterred by this they carried on with their task returning, on completion, to the front room to open a window in order to dispel the final significant area of smoke logging. As they did this I waited on the other side of the glass seeking to gain from them a status report of the fire and to confirm the successful completion of their search.

Seeing my crouching figure Mickey opened the window and grabbed my arm to draw me closer to him, enabling me to hear his report through the muffling effect of his BA mask. These actions were as one and resulted in me inhaling the incredibly nauseous smell which came out of the room. Finding myself in Mickey's firm grasp I was unable to make as rapid an exit from the window opening as I wanted.

Eventually breaking free and reeling back gasping and gagging from the stench, which seemed to simultaneously hit the back of my throat and nostrils, I noticed others nearby reacting with hands to mouths and cries of "What the **** is that smell?" Mickey and Chris oblivious to any problem were confused by my reaction and so proceeded outside to establish what was going on.

It was as they emerged that the first clue to the source of the odour showed itself. Covering much of their boots and fire fighting trousers was a gooey white substance. They quickly both found themselves on the receiving end of a deluge of water from high-pressure hose reels and a rain of unsupportive comments from their colleagues.

Confused, and now in what they considered to be clean air, they removed their facemasks and in an instant they finally understood the reaction of those around them and in turn took up the cry of "What the **** is that?"

Supplying lighting to the scene all was revealed. It appeared that the house had been empty for some time but, for some reason unfathomable by us both at the time and subsequently, the previous occupiers had left behind them a large amount of cartons and plastic bottles of milk strewn across much of the floor of the house! This had, as maybe expected after several weeks in a warm unventilated house, not just gone off but congealed to a consistency similar to that of cold runny rice pudding.

Still secure within its containers this was not much of a problem. Such containers stood little chance of remaining intact under the fire fighting boots of two large firefighters on a determined search mission and so burst covering the floor as well as our intrepid duo.

A great deal of cleaning and decontamination of kit and equipment took place on return to station but it seemed to those who had attended to be a long time before the smell was finally forgotten.

A further incident with out of date drink that is still clear in my mind occurred on the New Years Eve of 1986. The call came in just before midnight and I left my wife to welcome in the New Year with the then favourite TV celebrity. Such are the sacrifices of a retained firefighter's partner!

The call was to a fire in a derelict house and whilst the crew were dealing with it I became thirsty and pulled from under the backseat of the cab of the fire engine a large bottle of orange juice we always kept for such occasions.

It was a dark night so I couldn't see into the bottle but confident of its contents I took a deep swig. It was only as something large soft and squishy hit the back of my throat that I realised I may have made an error! Quickly spitting out this strange substance I examined the contents of the bottle under torch light. The orange juice had been half consumed, probably back in the previous late summer, and had floating on it a thick green layer of mould which I had almost swallowed.

Naturally I was concerned at what this may do to my health and I shall be ever grateful to the gentlemen who appeared from a nearby house. He had been celebrating the New Year and kindly insisted that I partook of a drink from his bottle of whisky, for medicinal reasons only of course. To the end of my fire fighting days this squishy memory always came back to me when drinking from a bottle on a fire call.

**Children.**

Boys will be boys goes the saying and certainly when it came to responding to incidents not just involving but 'caused' by children then boys provided a long list over the years, indeed I can only recall one incident initiated by a girl!

Our earliest example of this trait occurred in the early hours of New Year's morning in 1985. A call came through to a young lad with his arm firmly wedged through the letter box on the front door of his house. For several years his parents had been in the habit of hanging a key on a length of string on the inside of the door. It was not, for security reasons (!), hung to dangle just behind the letter box but off to one side where little Johnny could reach through for it and let himself in.

This apparently worked well for several years but then came the day when Johnny was no longer so little! Johnny hadn't used this method of entry for a while and so hadn't noticed how much he'd grown. The young arms once so slender and bony were now developing muscles. He hadn't noticed that is until this, what was to be the last, occasion.

Johnny and the family were returning in the early hours after seeing in the New Year with friends. He had gone on ahead of the rest of the family and upon arrival at the front door finding himself keyless resorted to his standby procedure. Armed with the knowledge that not having done this for a while it had always been an easy thing to do! He proceeded to push his arm through the letter box, and pushed and pushed until realising he wasn't going to reach the string gave up. He then tried to extract his arm, without success. The rest of his family arrived and though able to get in, for Mum had a key, no matter how hard they tried they could not release our unfortunate Johnny. So it was that we were summoned.

Both Johnny and his family were embarrassed by the situation and this was not helped by the arrival of a big shiny fire engine with blue lights flashing outside their house. Followed shortly afterwards by a similarly lit police car containing a bored local bobby who had come along for something to do. This certainly had the neighbour's curtains twitching!

We reassured the family that calling us out was the right thing. Then picking out a particularly large saw discussed loudly amongst ourselves just where on the lads arm to commence cutting. Before both he and his Mum went completely white we produced a small spanner and unbolted the letterbox from the door.

Moving our operation to the kitchen we used a good supply of washing up liquid and were able to release Johnny's well soaped arm from the unwelcome appendage, much to the relief of all concerned. Finally and to make up a little for our earlier humour we bolted the letter box back into place on the door. With our customers still somewhat embarrassed but happy it was time for us to depart but not before we discussed one further issue.

This family lived next door to one of our firefighters and he pointed out that rather than call us all out they could have just rung his doorbell and he would have been happy to have helped. Sheepishly they replied that they didn't want to do this as they didn't want to disturb him. We good naturedly pointed out that instead they had actually disturbed both him and 14 others!

**Trees and Boys**

Boys often love to climb trees and it seems surprising that we were only ever called to one incident of a 'Boy stuck up a tree'. Well it did make a change from a cat! The lad in question had bravely climbed up but then when spotted by his mum his sense of valour deserted him and in a mist of tears convinced her waiting impatiently below that he was well and truly stuck! Following her call we were soon in attendance and after helping him down from his perch via our ladder he seemed no worse for wear. Although this may well have changed once his mother got him home.

Another lad we were called to firmly stuck in a tree when we arrived was also unable to move, though this time not from any lack of courage. The tree had him firmly in its grasp. The poor chap had been standing in the branch shaped 'Y' of a small tree when he slipped and the fork of the 'Y' sprung around his leg grasping him painfully in it. On this occasion when he noticed the saw we were carrying we quickly reassured him that his leg was in no danger as it was for the tree and not him.

Following a swift appraisal of the situation we did not make use of the saw as with a large firefighter pulling on each limb of the tree fork we sprang it apart and out the lad's leg popped. Apart from some soreness he was none the worst for wear.

### Tri-County Call

Located as we were close to the borders of three counties it was often the case that we would be called into either Berkshire or Surrey. This was to assist them or to respond as the first pump to an incident on their fire ground when they were occupied elsewhere. A cross border agreement was in place between each county fire service to enable this to happen, though not always used. There was one particularly unique occasion when we trudged across all three counties to deal with a fire.

It was a warm summer evening and we were called to an undergrowth fire. On arrival we found it was not that big but nevertheless required extinguishing. It was located in a field on the Berkshire side of the River Blackwater in Blackwater. The river at this point formed the county boundary between Berkshire and Hampshire.

The location of the fire was a few metres from the river bank but on the opposite side of the field and several hundred metres away from the nearest access point to it. Being quite muddy in places I had no intention of having the pump drive across this. We found we could position the pump close to the river on the Hampshire side and so parked there and sought out the nearest bridge by which to cross.

Walking along the Hampshire bank we eventually came to the main A30 road bridge and made our crossing. The river at this point had become the boundary between Hampshire and Surrey so crossing here took us into Surrey. We now walked along the Surrey bank back towards the scene of the fire crossing on our way to it a ditch which marked the boundary of Berkshire and Surrey.

Eventually we arrived at the fire which was still flaring up from time to time. We now called across the river to our pump operator, LFF John Hicks, still with the pump on the Hampshire side. We asked him to throw across the hose reel which we could pull over and with it connected to the pump in Hampshire fight the fire in Berkshire.

It was at the point of throwing the hose across that John found it simply too heavy to throw directly and so he had, he thought, a brainwave. By tying a length of rope to the end of the ceiling hook, this is like a long wooden pole with a point and hook at one end and used primarily for pulling down ceilings, hence the name, he could then throw this like a harpoon across the river. With us having one end of the line he would tie the other to the hose reel and we could pull it across.

With the line successfully attached to the 'harpoon' John gave it a mighty heave and we all watched mesmerised as the missile arched through the still evening air and landed perfectly in the centre of the river and well out of our reach!

Undaunted John was all for trying again but a more common sense, though wetter for some, approach was employed. John stepped into the shallows of the river and waded out as far as he safely could then, with our most junior crew member reciprocating from the other side, threw the line, this time without the harpoon attached, where it was grabbed

39

and the hose reel hauled over. The fire, which by now had got so bored waiting it had almost gone out on its own, was now successfully extinguished. To the end of his career John always insisted that a second throw of the harpoon would have been successful, and we always insisted that it wouldn't!

This event demonstrates the problem solving skills required of a firefighter. There were many occasions over the years where standard equipment was very successfully used in scenarios never expected of it to overcome the problems and challenges we encountered. Such an approach was called practical firemanship which called for initiative, imagination and good equipment knowledge. We regularly practised this during our regular training sessions and exercises.

**Medical Scare**

By the end of my time with Hampshire Fire & Rescue Service the threats posed to emergency workers by such diseases as AIDS and Hepatitis were well documented. Processes and procedures to deal with these threats and their possible consequences had been created and in the event of such a threat being encountered were carefully followed. This had not always been the case as the following story demonstrates.

Late one evening in the early autumn of 1987 we were called to an RTA on a local road. This involved a young lady who following a collision between her car and another was quite seriously trapped. Although not too seriously injured there was a certain amount of blood around as we released and carefully lifted her into the waiting ambulance.

Cleaning up the scene we followed our standard procedures of washing down any contaminated equipment as well as where needed ourselves. We returned to the station but on arrival were phoned by our control with the disturbing news that the RTA victim had informed the hospital that she was a carrier of the Hepatitis B virus.

At the time this meant very little to us and clearly from their reaction it meant little to the staff of our control room. They decided to be better safe than sorry and told us to stay on station. A vehicle would be sent to pick us up and take us to hospital for medical checks. Naturally we were somewhat concerned by this. Concern which was greatly increased when a further call was received from control informing us that we were not to be in contact with the driver of the vehicle! He would post the vehicle keys through the letter box of the station and then once he had departed we could use this to take ourselves to the hospital.

Following these instructions it was with some apprehension that 6 firefighters presented themselves to the emergency team at our nearest hospital in by then the early hours of the morning. They had been pre-warned of our arrival and so were suitably prepared, not as it turned out there was much to prepare for. A quick discussion with a doctor confirmed we had all worn our protective clothing including gloves. Then a check over for any open cuts or abrasions and we were reassured that all was well.

We then learned that Hepatitis B is communicated by body fluids not airborne. Although there was sense in being cautious we were concerned and disappointed how little knowledge there was at that time of this virus within the brigade.

Such issues are now far better understood. It is then somewhat incredulous that although firefighters are recommended to have a jab against this debilitating disease it is not free and the cost is met by the firefighter who in turn is unable to reclaim this expense from the fire service!

# Chapter 4

## It's The People Who Made the Station

The stories in this book contain the names of many of the firefighters who served in the first 25 years of Yateley Fire Station. All members of the station contributed much to their community by providing the cover to ensure the fire engine was able to respond when called and subsequently performed their duties well under often difficult conditions.

A few specific stories of these firefighters are produced here. My first thoughts are with those members who have since leaving sadly passed away.

FF Alan Fulcher. Alan was a big strong guy who also served as a retained firefighter at Fleet and Hartley Wintney fire stations before moving to Devon where he worked fulltime for the ambulance service. Tragically one day he collapsed and died from a massive heart attack, just as he had finished working on a heart attack victim. Part of the legacy he left at the station was the following story.

One particularly hot night Alan was working in a crew dealing with a fire which had in the dry conditions spread from the undergrowth into peat laden ground. These fires always proved difficult to fully extinguish and required a great deal of water. A mobile dam had been erected and was being filled. It was just about full as Alan and Danny Randall leant against it passing the time of day. Alan asked Danny if he was hot and he had hardly answered yes before Alan had grabbed him and he found himself tipped upside down over the edge of the dam and fully immersed in cold water, much to the amusement of the remainder of the crew and others watching, though not to a certain officer who walked away shaking his head!

Alan also had his serious side and his knowledge of first aid was hugely useful to both us and the many RTA victims we encountered, including the motorcyclist who drove into the side of the fire engine whilst Alan was driving and sustained a broken leg for his error.

FF John Bentley. John just loved the job. An early member of the crew he was completely reliable and would follow orders to the letter. Although away from the incidents he could 'talk the hind legs off a donkey' if he felt strongly about a particular subject.

When a medical problem was found he had no option but to retire. I remember this difficult occasion well for as he was informing me of this sad news in my office a call came through to a car on fire. He pleaded with me to let him be part of the crew for one last time. Such calls were routine for us and though hesitant I agreed and off he went.

Once the fire was out he asked LFF John Hicks who was in charge of the incident to allow him to drive back to the station. As he drove tears rolled down his cheeks and having parked the pump in the station he disappeared home saying very little to anyone. John underwent significant surgery but sadly died of a heart attack one day whilst playing cricket, a sport he loved. He had just been given out by the umpire and as he strode off he collapsed and died, out for the last time but certainly not forgotten. We were proud to provide a guard of honour at his funeral.

As the years have passed some of us inevitably hit the age to retire and by the end of our first 25 years only Danny Randall and I remained from the original fifteen raw recruits who met on the first day of training back on August 3rd 1980. Since my retirement only Danny remained and I am delighted that he was chosen to take my place as the new officer in charge.

FF Paul Atkinson. Paul left us with many memories but few are printable, except for the following story of his wedding.

On the great day all the firefighters assembled at the church to attend the service and form an arch of raised fire fighting axes for the bride and groom to process under as they left the church. They would then mount a circa 1930's open fire engine hired especially for the occasion to transport them to the reception at the fire station.

The ceremony commenced and was progressing well. Then suddenly the peace of the occasion was shattered by the high pitched bleeping of a multitude of pagers. The previously designated members of the 'on duty crew' then leapt from their seats and rushed out. This action caused some consternation for the vicar and he quietly pointed out to the happy couple that numbers of their guests seemed to be running away! Reassured that this was not as uncommon as he may have thought he continued.

Arriving at the station we found we were being sent to attend a domestic garage fire on a local estate. LFF John Hicks drove that day. It was common practice that although the remainder of the crew would be dressed in fire kit upon attending an incident the driver would, preferring to drive in shoes rather than large heavy fire boots, dress at the incident. Normally not a problem as the driver acting also as the pump operator subsequently remained with the fire engine. Thus the urgency of his need for protective clothing was not as great as that of the remainder of the crew.

Once in attendance we found the incident to be small involving rubbish inside a garage of slab concrete construction. A short squirt from a hose reel dealt with it. As we returned to the pump we were greeted by the sight of the smartest turned out firefighter to ever attend a fire. John seeing how little work was required instead of dressing in fire kit and risk creasing his wedding clothes operated the pump in his best suit complete with carnation button hole. This certainly impressed many residents of the local neighbourhood who had been attracted by our sirens.

We returned directly to the church in time to add more colour to the wedding photographs before returning to the station especially decorated for the occasion.

FF Bill Robbins. When Bill retired we lost another hard worker who could be totally relied upon to perform well whatever the call. He was a quiet man who I only ever saw make one mistake. It was in our early days when we were training and had yet to be allowed out on the public. Bill missed his footing during a drill where he was climbing up the inside of the practice tower. He fell from the second to the first floor but suffering no injury he bounced up as though nothing had happened whilst his colleagues seeing him fall feared the worst! From a manager's perspective the only problem I had with Bill was to stop him working, especially cleaning and tidying the station. Like many others he just enjoyed the whole job.

FF John Dean. John having been with us from the start retired after deservedly gaining his twenty year long service and good conduct medal. I am particularly grateful to John for the help and advice both he and Bill Robbins gave me as we all became involved with the Retained Firefighters Union (RFU). One of our better drivers, me being the worst, or so I was often told by my crew, John did however manage to demolish the station doors, not just once but twice! He also on one occasion benefited by having the letters L and R daubed on the windscreen following the occasion he turned right instead of left on the way to a call.

FF John Chivers. A big man in every way he became a legend for his driving skills, so much so that many years after he retired drivers who had to take more than two attempts to drive the pump into the station were told "John Chivers would have done that in one!"

FF Norman Gibson. I know that Norman has a vivid memory of the time when attending a roof fire he found himself inside a bungalow under the open loft hatch. He had just been hosing water on to the fire overhead and had taken a step to one side when part of the roof collapsed and a huge pile of tiles poured through the loft opening onto the spot where he had been standing.

Others of us prefer to remember the time he had just refilled a dry powder extinguisher, a dusty unpopular job. He had performed this kneeling down and as he attempted to stand he placed his hand down on the nearest thing available to push himself up, the plunger on top of the extinguisher. So setting it off again! An excellent firefighter we were all sorry to see him leave.

FF David Garwood. Although David only joined us in 2003 his tales of the girls he met were always enjoyable. In particular the time we were performing a Christmas charity collection at Blackbushe Airport. A young lady saw him and after a few moments recognised him from a summer Spanish holiday. He agreed that they had met and remembered at the same time it was she who was topless in the photo he had shown us on his return. We all said hello and that we'd enjoyed seeing her before, at which point she went very red and disappeared into the crowd.

Just after David joined we asked him to check the dipstick on top of the pump, clambering up he spent some time looking around but confessed he could not find it. We of course told him it was easy as we could see the dipstick from here, it was him! I have no doubt he will continue to serve his community well for years to come.

FF Kim Blunt. Kim was the first female member of the station. She had moved up from Dorset where she had been a retained firefighter and so transferred across to us. In my early years I did not believe that women could make good firefighters. Kim proved me completely wrong.

Kim brought a whole new dimension and added value to our work. Whenever we had a woman or child victim to help Kim's presence and social skills made a big difference whilst at the same time she performed all the duties expected of any firefighter and performed them well. She quickly proved herself to be a significant asset to the station and always able to give as good as she got with the inevitable good natured ribbing we all enjoyed from our fellow crew mates. Especially after the time she fell off her bicycle when responding to the station and ended up prostrate at the feet of one of her colleagues!

FF Steven Geen. Another later recruit to the station, I remember well the evening we had him testing railway warning horns. These were used during incidents on a railway line and blown as a warning of trains approaching. We sent Steven walking off from the station with the horns telling him to blow them when a certain distance away. He then returned but we said he had been far too close and to go even further away. We kept this coming and going up for a while before he realised he had become yet another victim of our humour. Steven became the shop manager of a well known confectioner and was soon answering to the name of Willie Wonka, or similar, from his crew mates.

FF Ryan Pratley. Although I have already mentioned Ryan elsewhere the following must be told. Ryan had been a retained firefighter with us for several years before in 2005, and after many disappointments, he finally achieved his ambition and became a whole time firefighter. So well did he perform on his whole time recruits course that he won the silver axe for the most outstanding recruit, something he richly deserved and that reflected well on the training LFFs John Hicks and Danny Randall had given him during his time with us. We were all delighted to see him return to Yateley and carry on his retained responsibilities as well as serving on a fulltime station in his 'proper' job.

FF Ian Stones. Ian had several personal challenges the most obvious being that of his height, or lack of it. In the Watch Room of the station, where all fire kit was hung ready to be grabbed at a moment's notice, were a row of hooks upon which the bags containing the firefighters' helmets were hung. These were around six foot off the ground and whilst this was no problem to anyone else being vertically challenged Ian found them hard to reach and so placed his bag on a lower hook. The rest of the station personnel thought this untidy and would quickly relocate the bag to its correct and higher position. The positive aspect of this was that the jumping Ian had to do to retrieve his bag certainly contributed to his fitness.

Being on the short side can be a very positive advantage on the fire ground. If ever we were confronted with a small opening through which we needed to gain an entry Ian quickly became very popular. An excellent example of this was when we were called to deal with a most unusual entrapment involving an elderly lady and two doors.

Mrs Evans was an elderly lady of average size and like any other householder knew her home well. Or so she thought. Late one afternoon she decided to visit the local shops so donning a coat and picking up her bag prepared to leave. The original front door of her house was recessed in from the front wall. Like many of her neighbours houses at some time the recess had had a further door added flush with the front wall thus providing a small alcove of about 20 inches deep. This gave additional insulation from noise and cold to the inner hallway. Both doors opened inwards.

This arrangement caused no problem for many years until the day Mrs Evans forgot her door keys. Unfortunately Mrs Evans only realised her mistake when she had closed the first, or original, front door behind her. Even more unfortunate was that she had not, as she normally did, opened the new front door and so found herself firmly stuck in the space between the doors. The space into which the new front door would normally open but was unable to do so as she was already occupying it! There was simply nowhere to go and calling for help was the only option.

She managed to partially open the new front door enough to get her arm around and wave whilst at the same time calling for help. Luckily after sometime she attracted the attention of some passing schoolgirls who, once they understood the dilemma, dialled 999 for the fire brigade. After a few minutes we duly arrived to find a very embarrassed Mrs Evans and quickly agreed with her that she was indeed well and truly stuck! But she could relax as we would certainly be able to help her escape from her predicament.

Now contrary to what some might say when dealing with any incident we tried very hard to ensure that we caused the absolute minimum amount of damage to resolve whatever problem we are presented with, and preferably none at all! For the problem we had here we really did not want to simply break down doors and leave her a serious and expensive security repair problem unless absolutely unavoidable.

Whilst reassuring Mrs Evans we began to survey the property for open windows or other means of entry. Being very security minded she had made sure these were at a minimum, then upon closer inspection we noticed a small window, which as it turned out was the downstairs loo. This was of the louvre type and by careful use of a screwdriver we managed to prise out the glass and create a small opening of about, well as we all agreed, of about Ian's size.

With plenty of words of encouragement and only a comparatively small amount of physical pushing our Ian became the hero of the day squeezing himself through the opening. Fortunately on dropping through the window he missed the loo itself and within a very short time had the inner door unlocked and open allowing a very relieved Mrs Evans back into her home. He then opened the new front door and presented himself to us flushed with success.

FF Antony White. Having a fulltime job as a postman Antony naturally got up early every morning to ensure we had our post on time. Unfortunately put him in a warm room in the evening, for example at a training lecture, and sleep was certain to follow. When this did occur however it resulted in finding a new, some say better, use for a pool cue!

As one of our drivers Antony was from time to time entrusted with the big red fire engine. Now this beast weighs 12 tons fully laden and

49

obviously, to most people, the idea of trying to drive it over a narrow wooden bridge out in the middle of Yateley Common really would be a bridge too far. But not to our Antony! However soon after the heavy rescue truck eventually managed to tow us out of the splintered wood and other assorted debris he finally agreed that yes this did now seem to be a dumb idea!

How he found the time from his post office job to provide us with the excellent amount of hours of availability that he did was always a mystery to me. It was a pleasure to have him as a crew member.

FF Nigel White. Probably our best driver, which is as it should be as he drove a 32 ton lorry for a living. Fortunately when driving the fire engine he never drove over and crushed any parked cars as he did in his fulltime job! Nigel contributed hugely to the community safety activities of the station by organising and running, with notable help from at one time or another almost all others of the crew, visits to the station and subsequent fire safety talks to hundreds of local children who visited as Cubs, Brownies and other youth groups over the years.

LFF John Hicks. When John retired his fellow firefighters were concerned that he would become bored. To help him cope with this possibility, and whilst he was saying his goodbyes elsewhere, we took his bicycle, the one he had used for many years to respond to the station from home, and dismantled it down to its last nut and bolt. We then took great trouble to pack all the parts into several cardboard boxes. At the end of the evening a formal presentation to him of these boxes was made. As he opened his farewell gift all of those present agreed that it was the first time ever we had known him lost for words!

John had enjoyed many events on that bicycle including the time when during some terrible winter weather it followed an icy rut in the frozen snow depositing him into a road side snow bank! On another occasion, when John had not responded fast enough to crew the pump to a large blaze in a nearby school, he cycled to the incident for a look. Being distracted by the conflagration in front of him he failed to notice the school long jump pit and, shortly after the front wheel buried itself in the deep sand, was catapulted over the handle bars of his trusty steed!

Despite these mishaps John served his community well for 24 years and all of the stations' recruits, in whom he took great pride in providing with a huge amount of personal training in so many aspects of their new role, owed him a huge debt of gratitude.

Station Cleaner David Newman. David (or Norman as a certain forgetful firefighter kept calling him) was one of the original group but during training decided that wearing BA was not for him. Instead he's held the very important role of station cleaner since the station opened and all of us were always glad to see his happy smiling face and hear his chirpy cheerful voice whenever we strode in all over his freshly cleaned floor.

Nicknames are a common feature in the fire service and despite in the 1990's an HR department trying to ban them they still are. They are invariably used in an affectionate way and certainly not malicious. Although the circumstances they are sometimes earned can embarrass the individual. Take Flipper for example.

This firefighter had not been with us long and was very keen. One evening on responding to our pagers we found ourselves sent to a flood threatening several properties. As we arrived I stepped down from the pump and noticed something odd. There seemed to be water everywhere and clearly houses were in danger of flooding. But I could not understand why from the middle of the dark wet road protruded the rear half of a car at about 45°! A nearby disgruntled police officer quickly enlightened me. "There I was" he said "Successfully directing the traffic around this crater in the middle of the road", caused by the force of water from a broken main. "When this guy simply ignored my signals and drove head long into it". The crater had by then filled with water.

It turned out that "this guy" was one of the crew responding to his pager trying to reach the station via the flooded road. He had seen the directions of the police officer but thought it was simply a puddle in front of him and decided he would make faster progress going through rather than around it. He was wrong! After this dolphin like performance he was given the well earned name of Flipper!

Many others contributed to the success of the station and all names of those who served their community in its first 25 years are shown at the end of this book. Each have their own memories and their own stories to tell.

**Those who Contributed from Outside.**

I have been privileged to meet many real characters during my years with the fire service but one of the earliest and one from whom I learnt so much about running a retained fire station was the highly respected Officer in Charge, Crowthorne Fire Station, Royal Berkshire Fire Brigade, Sub Officer Peter Geldzetzer BEM.

Pete attended numerous fires in the Yateley area during his fire service career and a favourite story he would tell was as follows.

During the long hot summer of 1976 Pete and his colleagues from Crowthorne were often to be found dealing with undergrowth fires on Yateley Common. Working hard on one occasion they had managed to create a fire break and stopped a fire from spreading when suddenly from amongst the flames appeared a fox.

Its brush tail was aflame as it ran from the conflagration across the fire break and into the cover of a dry unburnt area of bracken and gorse. In doing so it set a trail of fire behind it doubling the work load of the already hard pressed firefighters.

Pete and I always got on well and I count myself fortunate that this was the case. I had not been operational long when we met for the first time at a fire. One of my first whereas by then Pete had lost count of the number of incidents he had attended. Perhaps it was my willingness to learn and recognition of his experience that started us off so well but whatever it was he was one of the people I have respected most in my time fire fighting.

Pete was one of the last firefighters we knew as a 'smoke eater' a term used to describe guys who did not always bother with breathing apparatus and could quite happily work unaided in what I would consider to be a very smoky atmosphere. Not in hindsight the safest thing to do but it was their choice.

My clearest memory of Pete which underlined this was when both our crews attended and supported each other at a property fire. Our breathing apparatus teams had worked hard and after they had extinguished the fire Pete was keen to get inside and investigate its cause. So in we went. The room where the fire had been though by now ventilated was still very smoky and in a short time I was crouching down at floor level searching for the cleanest air. Looking up I saw this vivid image of Pete not only suffering no ill effects but also puffing away on his ever ready 'after the fire' pipe. It was too much for me and I left coughing with eyes streaming. Though I insisted afterwards that what set me off was not the smoke from the fire but the acrid smoke given off by the tobacco he loved!

Amazingly, and pleasingly, Pete even in his 70's does not appear to have suffered any ill effects from either type of smoke, though he did give up the pipe sometime ago.

There is one story about Pete I cannot leave out and like most good stories it is absolutely true, or so I am assured.

Pete like many of us loved being a retained firefighter, he had dedicated many years of his life to it often at a cost to his business and to his family. This latter fact being something that the families of most retained firefighters have experience of and something none of us took for granted.

Pete was a realist and knew that time was marching on and though he wasn't getting any younger he wanted to pass his last medical and get a few more years in before retirement age over took him. Until the late 1990's the use of any form of visual aids by firefighters was forbidden, even reading glasses, thus to fail an eyesight test during a routine medical could result in the person concerned having to leave the fire service on a medical discharge.

Fortunately like many outdated attitudes and traditions within the fire service good sense eventually prevailed with overdue and welcome changes sweeping much of such rubbish away. But such changes had not happened in Pete's time and he was worried. To him his eyesight just wasn't what it was and he knew he had to do something, so he did.

I shall now introduce Les P, a Leading firefighter at Crowthorne Fire Station and in many ways Pete's right hand man, he was for many years Pete's trusted friend and it is to him I am indebted for the following story.

One afternoon Les received a phone call from Pete.
"Hi Les you busy" Pete began.
"No why what's up" Les replied.
"Well let's go out for a drive"
"Ok"
"Oh and could you bring those binoculars you have with you" added Pete.
"What for?"
"Oh nothing" said Pete, "See you in a while"

This set Les thinking but as he told me "I just thought Pete wanted to look at the aeroplanes taking off from Heathrow"

Pete duly arrived and casually suggested they take a drive over to Slough. Les took this as an indication that his suspicions were correct as Slough is directly under the Heathrow flight path. So off they set.

Arriving in Slough Pete asked Les "You know the multi-storey car park in the town centre?" "Yes" replied Les, "Well let's take a drive up there".

This lay to rest any remaining suspicions Les had as he knew that there was a fine view of the aircraft flying overhead to be had from the top floor of this car park. But they didn't get that far. As Les was driving on to the third floor Pete suddenly called out.

"Pull over here". Les was now completely at a loss as to what was going on, but Pete very soon enlightened him.

"Now" said Pete getting out of the car "Grab your binoculars and follow me". Reaching the edge of the car park Pete began to explain himself.

"Right, you see that building opposite" "Yes" said Les.

"Well on the third floor, the window fourth in from the right" said Pete pointing to it "is the room where they hold the fire brigade medicals"

"So" stuttered a by now bewildered Les.

"So on the far wall of the room is the eye chart they use in these medicals. Now take a look through your binoculars and tell me what the chart says, I'll write them down and memorise them for the eye test I'm having as part of my medical here tomorrow morning".

Les was amazed but as I said he was a true friend and not wanting to let Pete down he raised his binoculars to the indicated window and commenced to comply with what Pete wanted.

"Pete" said Les,

"Yes" said Pete pen and paper poised.

"I understand what you want but can't see a thing"

"Why not?" said Pete "Problem with the bino's?"

"No" replied Les "The window is frosted glass!"

We should now leave the story and Pete's reaction to this news but I am pleased to say that he need not have worried, his concerns proved groundless as he passed the medical and went on to complete his time and onto a happy retirement with the deserved award of a British Empire Medal for services to his community.

I have already said that Pete provided me with lots of useful advice for which I am truly grateful, one piece of information he provided me with proved not just useful but financially very advantageous.

One night over a late night beer with him, something we used to share a couple of times a month. Pete told me of a new leaflet that Royal Berkshire Fire Brigade had introduced packed with advice and contact information for victims of house fires on what to do after the fire. This was to be given, prior to departure of the fire crew, to a householder who had suffered as useful advice on how to start the recovery process. This was a big improvement upon the then common practice of simply driving off and leaving the poor victim, usually in shock to sort themselves out without any help.

As we chatted we both agreed what a simple but good idea it was and I thought little more about it for a few weeks, until one day the weekly Hampshire Fire Brigade post arrived on my desk. In this post was a leaflet announcing a competition being held by Hampshire County Council for all employees called 'Bright Ideas'. This was a suggestion scheme for improving the council services to the customer.

Firefighters were entitled to enter as the fire brigade was part of the county council and technically we were employed by them. I was about to throw this leaflet in the bin when a thought struck me. If an idea was good in Berkshire it could be considered a bright one in Hampshire. I completed the entry form included on the leaflet with a description of 'my' idea and after sending it off promptly forgot about it. Until that is a surprise letter dropped through my letter box telling me I had won a £50 prize in the first round of the competition and 'my' idea was being put forward into the final round. This offered a £1000 prize.

Delighted to receive the cash I thought little more about the chances of winning more and again forgot about it. Then one day I received a call from a senior fire officer. He asked if I would be attending the council reception where the winner would be announced. Being particularly busy at work at this time I said no. He persisted and said brigade wanted me to attend in full uniform to represent them. I agreed to participate and although at the last minute I almost pulled out through pressure of work arrived at the event with a view to enjoying a glass of wine and with the presentation completed heading off home as soon as possible.

The ceremony of announcing the winner commenced with the top three being given in the traditional reverse order. Suddenly to hear my name being called out in joint first place left me speechless, not a common occurrence as those who know me will confirm. I had shared the top prize, with I recall a librarian, though the share was not for some reason even as I received £800 and he £200!

Suddenly I was propelled forward to the stage to receive the cheque from the leader of the council. Only at this point did I spot the senior officer who had phoned me. He had, it turned out, been aware of the identity of the winner for some time hence his insistence on my attending. Several photos and local press and radio interviews followed before I was able to get away.
It only struck me on the drive home that the idea perhaps though regarded by Hampshire County Council as a bright one wasn't quite an original. Nevertheless they were happy and indeed so was I.

That night though I knew I had to do the right thing with Pete and over a beer I let him know of my good fortune, he thought it hilarious and accepted the beer I bought him as thanks. Yes I did offer more but he wouldn't hear of it, such is the friend he was. I'm pleased to add that Hampshire Fire Brigade took up the idea and produced the first of a series of leaflets for fire victims who I understand found them very useful.

## Who's Beautiful Launderette?

Then there was Tim, a modern thinking officer, who was with us one day at a fire in a local launderette. As was often the case we had dealt with the fire by the time of his arrival but a contribution to establishing the facts of how it started was welcome. As ever we were pleased to see him. The owner of the establishment was not at the scene and in this case the on site manager had little knowledge of the washing machines so we waited for the owner to arrive.

The shopping area where the launderette was located was not at its busiest but people were coming and going. Suddenly a car pulled up and parked adjacent to the launderette and a large man in his fifties emerged from it. "Ah" decided Tim, "This must be the owner." Striding up to the gentleman he shook him by the hand and formally introduced himself saying how sorry he was at the damage the shop had suffered. At this point the guy said "Interesting but nothing to do with me, I've just stopped to buy a paper from the newsagents!" A very red faced Tim withdrew with half stuttered apologies and to the background of not so stifled giggles from the assembled firefighters. Yet another little incident that has been recalled many times over a warm beer.

# Chapter 5

## Of Creatures Great and Small

Animal rescues have been a regular feature for us and the following are some of the more memorable ones.

### The Parrot Rescue

The month of May could often, dependent upon the amount of rain it brought, be a very busy one for us. Yateley being surrounded on almost all sides by common land any dry spell brought with it an increase in grass and gorse fires. Often ignited deliberately by some sad individual or accidentally by the army using various flares and other pyrotechnics during their war games.

The first Monday of May always saw our regular attendance at the Yateley May Day Fayre. The local community event of the year and one we were always keen to support. It was a day when we were pleased to receive long queues of sticky fingered children all eager to climb on board, and quite a few mums and dads as well. They loved to spin the steering wheel or probe the switches to test the siren, which somehow always became disconnected just after we arrived and reconnected as we departed.

Having attended the Fayre in 1987 we were back at the station removing the sticky finger marks from the cab when we received a call to what turned out to be a bizarre incident, but one with a successful outcome. It was to rescue a parrot stuck up a tree!

A short journey took us to the incident where we were met by Station Officer Sid Cole, a wholetime operational fire officer highly respected by all of us. On reporting to him Sid explained to me, as he puffed on his inevitable cigarette, that a parrot had escaped from its cage whilst it was being cleaned out. It had flown up into a large oak tree in the owner's garden, from where so far it had resisted all attempts to coax it down. Although a bright sunny day the owner was becoming increasingly concerned that the very valuable bird would not survive in the open as a frost had been forecast for that night.

Following a quick assessment we agreed that the best approach would be to pitch a ladder at the foot of the tree and ascending it 'encourage' the bird to flutter back to the safety of its cage, or at least to the ground where it could be easily captured. In hindsight although this seemed like a good plan no one had explained it to the parrot! However the owner assured us that its wings had been clipped and it couldn't fly, only flutter!

The ladder was pitched and a volunteer, my turn, began the ascent. It was about this time that a significant thought struck me. If the bird's wings had been clipped how then had it managed to fly up into the tree in the first place? We were to learn that maybe the wing clipping had not been completed as well as it could have been.

Once in place I took the approach of trying to scare the bird off its perch by arm waving and crawling out towards it along the bough it was resting on. The bird responded to this with a rather bored look. It simply walked further out along the tapering bough with an attitude of if you want me come and get me! For me to move further out along the bough was not an option, despite the encouragement from my crew below of "Come on yer woose", so we adopted a new tactic.

We carried on board a stock of cane chimney rods used usually with a hose attachment they are screwed together and pushed up inside chimneys on fire, enabling water to be applied direct to their fiery linings.

The crew screwed together four rods from this stock and I was presented from below with a pole of about 3 metres long with which to more directly encourage the bird to take its leap to safety. This action was

60

accompanied by a number of suggestions from the crew including the inevitable one of "Come on Colin you knock it off its perch and we'll catch it in this POLLYthene bag."

After careful manoeuvring of the pole the bird acknowledged it had had enough encouragement by deciding to jump rather than suffering an unfriendly poke and off it leapt. But to flutter down no! Indeed far from fluttering it spread its wings and flew serenely out above the heads of the milling throng below. On and on it flew out into the bright sky and heading not just out of the garden but also out of the county! Then just as it was about to achieve the status of a POLLYgone and disappear from view it began a U turn and, with me providing a running flap by flap commentary of its travels to those below, appeared to fly into a garden a couple of hundred metres or so to our right.

I quickly descended the tree and joined the owner, the other five firefighters of my crew, the fire engine, two police officers who had nothing better to do, in their police car and Sid as we moved the rescue scene to the area I had indicated. At the same time being quizzed by the inevitable gaggle of small children our appearance so often attracts as to 'Where's the fire mister?" Explaining we were seeking an escaped parrot seemed to disillusion them somewhat but they followed on in some numbers.

We searched the area I had indicated high and low for several minutes with no result until a call from one of the crew FF Martin Bone, a firefighter who was to go on to specialise in cat rescues, mostly because he was one of the few of us who really liked cats, drew my attention to an amazing sight of a gentleman with a parrot on his shoulder peering out at us from his lounge window. On seeing we had spotted him he ducked behind some curtains. The parrot however continued to peer at us from around them. I was totally bemused by all this but decided that a knock on the door and a quick chat would resolve things. Oh that it was to be that easy.

Upon knocking the door was opened by a lady who very pleasantly asked the nature of our business. I patiently explained all that had happened and asked her where the parrot I had seen a gentleman in the house shouldering had come from. She then went to explain at great length that they had lost a parrot themselves sometime ago when it had flown off. She asked me to describe the bird I was seeking.

Fortunately before I could reply a gentleman appeared in the hallway with 'the' parrot still perched upon his shoulder. He greeted us with a friendly smile and asked what it was we wanted. Patiently once more I described the recent events that had led us to his door and in doing so I made it clear I thought the bird he had was indeed the missing parrot. At which he pointed to the bird on his shoulder and would no doubt have completed his sentence of "What this one?" had the parrot not at that moment grabbed the pointed finger in its powerful beak. As the gentlemen dissolved in pain I announced that enough was enough. Our job of rescue was complete and that if he wanted to dispute the ownership of the bird then the 'other' owner and two police officers were outside and invited him to please take it up with them.

Clearing a path through the crowd now swollen by interested neighbours we returned to the station where with Sid we reviewed the whole silly scenario over a well earned beer. The parrot by the way was returned to its rightful owner, the original caller.

This would be a good time to write more about FF Martin Bone who served his community well during his time with us. Martin loved most animals and as already mentioned in particular, or so it seemed to us, cats! Indeed he developed a well earned reputation amongst us for his heroic rescues of our feline friends. The most memorable rescue though was one which almost ended in disaster. For the cat!

One Monday evening we were at the fire station as usual practicing, on this occasion putting up ladders, when a lady in some distress appeared.

She regaled us with the story of how her dear pussy was stuck at the top of a very tall pine tree and indeed had been since the previous day. At first I tried to explain that we did not respond to "cat stuck up a tree" incidents until requested to by the RSPCA and only then after they had visited the scene and assessed the situation.

This however seemed to distress her more and being a sucker for tears I decided that this could actually be a good training opportunity and a chance to put our much practiced ladder skills into use in a real situation and so agreed to take a crew along to see if we could be of help.

Upon arrival we found, just as the lady had described, a very tall pine tree. So tall in fact it would be a challenge for our 10.5 metre ladder to reach its top branches. Undaunted we gave it a try and the ladder team worked well managing to position the top of the ladder just a few feet below the, by now meowing loudly, pussy.

It was time now for someone to perform the rescue and sure enough without any hesitation up stepped Martin volunteering to climb up and see if he could reach the miserable moggy!

Climbing the ladder skilfully he soon found himself at its top but would need to free climb a few feet off of the ladder in order to get a hand on the animal. Reminding him that his life was far more valuable than the cat's I agreed he could carry on and he quickly ascended to the point where he could grab the cat and opening his fire tunic he secured, he thought, the beast inside it for the journey down.

All went well until he stepped back onto the ladder. The cat then became decidedly unhappy about sharing the multiple occupancy of Martin's tunic with him and started to struggle. Much to Martin's chagrin! Clutching his tunic and the unhappy occupant within to him he managed to arrest the movement and indeed stopped it from falling out from the tunic bottom. Though not fully. For from under the bottom of his tunic and between his legs the cat's tail appeared in an extremely phallic fashion. He quickly completed his descent, with much encouragement from his assembled crew mates, and the cat was returned to its grateful owner.

That story was not the only one that Martin contributed to the history of the station. Shortly after his wedding to the delightful Carol, the reception of which was held in the specially decorated pump bay at the station with the pump parked safely outside, Martin was a member of a crew attending an unpleasant RTA on the main road to Reading in Eversley.

There is always a great deal to do at such incidents but one of the most important jobs is to ensure the safety of those at the scene most commonly by stopping or at least closely controlling the traffic on the road. Preferably this is a task for the police but until their arrival it was one we regularly had to undertake.

On this occasion Martin was assigned this task and as ever was determined to carry it out to the full. It was I recall a particularly dark night. Martin stood squarely in the road ready to stop any traffic attempting to make its way through. To start with there was a lull in the traffic but not for long as around the bend appeared a very large articulated lorry. All fire and ambulance warning lights were fully deployed and repeatedly blinking out their blue warning message for all to see.

There was Martin, standing in the middle of the road clad in full fire kit and a regulation conspicuity jacket with his hand held aloft palm outwards in the customary STOP sign. The lorry driver seemed to hesitate, possibly distracted by the scene suddenly confronting him, before applying his brakes. The lorry came closer and closer to Martin. Then with all its brakes applied and its speed dropping dramatically the lorry shuddered in its attempt to halt, so much in fact that those working to extract the victim from the RTA were distracted by the noise.

Before them was the scene of Martin standing his ground! His hand held determinedly aloft and the lorry coming ever closer to him. Finally it stopped with Martin's hand almost pressed up against the windscreen.

Unfazed Martin gave the driver a nod and calmly turned to see everyone watching him. Dedicated or daft the reasons behind his action seemed to blur together and although he insisted he had time to jump out of the way those who watched the climax spellbound were never too sure!

Incidents involving animal rescues were a fairly common occurrence for us and usually the animal was pleased to see us. Not however on the occasion we were called to rescue a cat that had been 'stuck' on a rooftop for several days.

Following normal practice for such incidents the ladder was set up to the eaves of the house and a firefighter was volunteered to perform the rescue. On this occasion as he climbed the ladder and appeared in view of the cat it suddenly became very frightened and threw itself off the roof and into what seemed oblivion!

Fortunately it landed in a large bush, which broke its fall, and after tumbling through the branches it scampered away none the worse for its experience. This was a clear lesson for us to learn and in the future when faced with the same situation we always made sure the firefighter who ascended the ladder was not the ugly one!

Cats are notorious for requiring rescue by the fire service and we certainly had our share of them stuck up trees, on roofs, behind cupboards in fact anywhere they can get access to. Such rescues often left their mark and not always just on the memory as I personally have the scars to prove.

Late one evening we were called to rescue a cat which had somehow, only the cat seemed to know how, managed to clamber in and wedge itself behind some newly fitted kitchen units. It had been there for sometime and judging by the noise it was making was beginning to suffer. Upon examination of its precise location we were left with two choices, dismantle the new kitchen, the householder would then have the problem of reassembly and fitting, or just possibly someone with a long arm could reach down behind the units and grasp the poor creature. Being the one with the longest arms I started on the second option.

To enable me to squeeze my arm through the limited space between wall and kitchen unit I had to remove my glove. An action I was later to regret. By laying on top of the units and pushing and squeezing my arm into the available space I managed to just reach kitty. It was at this point that kitty reached out for me and promptly sank a set of claws into my bare hand and stayed hooked on!

Somewhat faster than I had entered I extracted my arm and hand with dear kitty still hanging on for dear life! As we reached the kitchen worktop level the cat twisted away and was free. Darting off as quickly as possible leaving me to remove the two claws it had left behind embedded firmly in my hand!

The owner seemed more interested in the welfare of their pet than my predicament but the rest of the crew as usual rallied round and searched all of the fire engine lockers to see if they could find any sympathy for me but to no avail! I though was just pleased to have had my anti-tetanus booster, it's an important issue in our job as you never know where some of these mucky firefighters have been.

In the early years of the station's history barn fires, barns that are full of straw usually fairly freshly cut, were regular events. As time progressed and our fire ground became more urbanised so there have been fewer barns to burn. Of all these fires the first was also for me the most memorable.

It was a Saturday evening in September 1982, a month after we had opened for business and still going through a very steep learning curve.

As a result of our training we were well versed in all the equipment available to us but very short of actual fire ground experience. Fortunately I believe we knew this and worked within ourselves whilst the experience was gained. Though occasionally a sharp lesson would be learnt or on this occasion two sharp lessons!

We received the call to a barn fire and on route we could see a tell tale column of black smoke marking our destination. Upon arrival we were confronted with a two-storey farm building with smoke and flame pouring from it. Or "well alight" as we firefighters would report such scenes.

The upper floor was open on three sides and piled high with hundreds of bales of hay many of which were directly involved in the fire. Below these was the ground floor which was partitioned off to create two animal pens containing young cattle. These beasts were becoming extremely agitated by what was occurring above them. Our priority, after our own safety, was the rescue of these poor creatures.

The initial challenge was to get close enough to release the latches and open the gates of the pens; the problem was that the radiated heat from the fire was preventing any normal approach. To solve this I had one of the crew direct a jet of water onto my back, the resultant spray then formed a water curtain isolating me from the heat of the fire. I managed to quickly open the pens and a few shouts encouraged the animals to get out of there. All that is except one! No amount of shouting would make this particular brute run for it, it simply stood shaking in the far most corner of the pen.

By now I was under the floor where the bales were located and so away from the radiated heat. Naturally I was concerned at the possibility of any collapse but quickly observed that the roof of the pens upon which the bales of hay were laid consisted entirely of reclaimed railway sleepers and so provided a good strong platform.

As a young lad I had been brought up on a diet of TV westerns and had learnt from my boyhood heroes just how to deal with an "ornery critter" like this heifer. All one had to do was to grasp the animal in a headlock and wrestle it down before simply dragging it out of harm's way, and so I did, or rather abjectly failed to do. Oh yes I secured the headlock in place, or so I naively thought. But this none impressed the animal which gave a flick of his, surprisingly for me, powerful neck and head and I was off, smacked against the hard breeze block wall of the pen!

As I picked myself up to consider my next move I was joined in the action by Pete Tarrant the then Officer in Charge of Hartley Wintney fire station. He and his crew had been sent on as an additional pump due to the type and size of the incident.

Now Pete, being more of a country boy than I, declared that the only way to deal with an animal like this was to "Punch it up the arse!" Fortunately smoke masked our activities from the outside as with the creature's tail in hand we chased the beast round and round the pen trying to do just that. Still the poor thing would not come out so it was time for plan C, or was it D by then. I went out and fetched a rope which we tied around the beast's neck, that's the heifer's not Pete's. Using most of the crew then we dragged it out to safety. Even then the 'fun' was not quite over as one firefighter in an attempt to calm the creature down sat astride it. Only for it to take off with him on its back! Although not for long!

Several hours later I learnt my second lesson of the day in a very smelly way.

Once bales of hay and straw have been subjected to fire and subsequently smoke they are worthless as animal feed as the animals will simply not touch it. This presents the farmer with a problem of disposal and often the best option in this case is to allow the fire, under fire service supervision, to burn itself out.

On this occasion though the structure of the barn could be saved by extinguishing the fire and so followed several hours of pitch forking out the burning bales whilst they were sprayed with water, all done by the firefighters present.

It was during this time that I allowed myself to become distracted and started to wander around the perimeter of the fire to check the progress of the hard working crews.

Walking past a seemingly solid building corner post of about 20ft high I suddenly realised it had taken that moment to topple over, and, much to my consternation, in my direction! In a desperate move to avoid being hit I threw myself out of the way as it came crashing down. Fortunately my landing was soft. Unfortunately this softness was offered by the large pile of not so fresh manure I had inadvertently thrown myself into. I quickly scrambled to my feet hoping that no one had observed my actions, but of course this was not to be and gales of laughter greeted me as covered in very smelly 'it', I hurriedly sought out a quiet corner to clean myself up!

It's not always the large animals that cause the most stress. Whilst attending a chimney fire in a local pub, normally one of our more pleasant calls, we encountered an unfriendly nest of wasps concealed under tiles on the roof who were clearly concerned we may be seeking to damage their home.

The incident had begun routinely enough. We had arrived to find that the cause of the fire was not actually in the chimney stack but in an extractor unit placed upon the top of the chimney where, when in operation, it ensured the chimney would 'draw' and so prevent the log fire below filling the pub with smoke.

Gaining access to the roof via our ladders we tackled the fire, with the expectation of bringing down the offending extractor unit to ground level so as to ensure it was completely out. It was as the water from our hose reels doused the flames that the two firefighters on the roof suddenly became aware of a great deal of buzzing as a multitude of wasps suddenly appeared around them. Naturally a rapid withdrawal to safety of firefighters then took place.

Following a quick review of the situation, or to give it its trendy modern name a 'dynamic risk assessment', two firefighters were volunteered to carry on dealing with the fire. They did so safe in the knowledge that their full fire kit of helmet, smoke hood, goggles, gloves, leggings and boots would afford them the protection they needed. Which it very nearly did, though not quite!

Off our heroes went and completed the task of extinguishing the fire whilst being constantly buzzed by the now very angry wasps. Despite some serious buzzing their protective clothing proved its worth and no stings were experienced. Thus it was that the firefighters triumphantly descended with the extractor unit to the safety of the ground.

It was as they began to discuss the incident that one of the firefighters, FF Ryan Pratley was attacked by two particularly determined wasps, not through his fire kit but underneath it! These adventurous insects had crawled up under Ryan's tunic and began to extract revenge in the only way they knew how. Without hesitation and amidst much cursing and leaping about Ryan quickly stripped to the waist whilst his crew members offered many words of advice and encouragement. None of sympathy, just advice and encouragement! 3 stings and two escaped wasps later peace was restored.

Our Ryan was at this time a fit young man in his early twenties and as the excitement subsided one could not help but notice the amount of young ladies, particularly the waitresses and barmaids from the pub who had assembled to watch the scene, or rather one semi-naked firefighter in particular. Clearly it was time to go!

Cat and dog rescues were relatively common for us over the years and despite our strenuous efforts there were occasions when we have not been successful. Several times we found dogs in smoke filled houses in which a fire had developed whilst their owners were out.

I well remember one particular incident when FF Norman Gibson as a member of a BA crew to enter a blazing house, appeared out of the smoke carrying a lifeless body which for one horrific moment I thought was a child with ginger hair. Instead it was a Red Setter dog. We tried hard as we did on all occasions this happened, to revive the poor thing but it was almost impossible to give mouth to mouth, or mouth to muzzle, to a dog.

There was also another sad occasion when dealing with the body of a dog which was lightened only by the black humour of LFF Chris Sayers. We had been sent to rescue a Jack Russell terrier. The poor creature had fallen into an underground water tank buried amongst undergrowth on the military training ground in our area.

Because of the remoteness of the incident it took us quite a while to find its location and when we did we peered in vain into the gloom of the tank for a sign of life. It was Chris who spotted the still bundle of fur floating at the far end of the tank and he who insisted upon calling it 'Bob' as we recovered the body through the murky water as a result of the way it proved so difficult to get hold of without it sinking into the depths.

Whether these animals appreciate our help is of course another matter though it was clear that the largest dog we were called to help most certainly did not.

Early one morning in August 1988 we were called to assist a St Bernard dog that had become stuck in a hole in the ground on Yateley common. Upon arrival we found that sure enough a large St Bernard had somehow slipped tail first into a foxhole. It was firmly stuck with just its formidable head and front legs protruding. We set about digging down

71

on both sides of the animal. Unfortunately for one firefighter his hard work was not appreciated by the dog which proceeded to demonstrate this by giving him a hefty bite on the arm. The dog's owner, who was also present, was a local doctor. Although it was agreed by the fire crew that he seemed much more concerned for his dog than for the firefighter's arm. Once the dog had calmed down digging recommenced and it was soon free. But it never did apologise to our bitten colleague.

Probably one of my most embarrassing animal incidents was the time we were called to a bonfire out of control in a garden. On attending we found that an aviary was also involved. Quickly extinguishing the fire I then discussed the incident with the householder, offering sympathy for the two budgerigars we had found in the ashes of the aviary. Three birds he sharply corrected me, "Er no we only found two" I offered "Well you need to count the one you are standing on!" he acidly pointed out. Embarrassed I lifted my foot and there was burnt budgie number three.

In the USA the traditional image of a fire station, or firehouse as they are known there, invariably includes a station mascot of a Dalmatian dog. Often portrayed as waiting patiently for the pump and his masters to return from a call.

No such animal ever resided at Yateley fire station but there is a creature whose successive generations have tolerated our presence, the 'station fox'. This is due in part no doubt to the actions of several well meaning, though misguided in some views, firefighters' habit of occasionally leaving food for them.

These foxes have periodically paid closer than welcome visits and even entered the station itself when a door was inadvertently left open. Resulting in the total disappearance of slippers, carried it is believed back to the depths of its earth by a good living fox. Plus the memorable occasion when a single expensive trainer shoe disappeared. When this was eventually located nearby it was found that the fox had taken full advantage of not just stealing it but, as is their habit, marking their territory in the normal very smelly way of urinating into it. Much to the dismay of the owner but to the usual merriment of the rest of the crew!

**Frying tonight!**

A frustrating call we occasionally experienced was that of being requested to attend an address and investigate a smell of burning. Frustrating because a long time could be spent sniffing the air and following our noses to track down the cause. Such causes, over the years, ranged from burnt milk to a common favourite of a damaged starter in a fluorescent lighting unit.

One pungent odour in particular took a long time to track down. We had been asked to attend a house in Eversley where the occupant smelt burning. On arrival there was a distinctive, but subtle, 'pong' about the property. We searched and searched to no avail. Then it was noticed that an external light was not working, so we focused our noses on this. Tracing the wiring back from the light to the nearest junction box we found the cause.

A hungry mouse had nibbled through the plastic insulation of the cable and literally fried itself. The poor creature was still in situ teeth firmly clamped into the wiring with a faint smoke rising from its body. Most notable were its eyes which bulged from its head and added to its expression of "What the **** was that!

We experienced two further examples of fried rodent and though years apart both identical and in the same place.

On each occasion we were called to smoke seen rising from around a wooden pylon holding a high voltage unit adjacent to Yateley common. This, as it turned out, also coincided with a power black out in the local area. Once in attendance we quickly found the cause.

A squirrel scampering from tree to tree had innocently attempted a leap between a live and neutral contact on the electrical unit but, unfortunately for the squirrel, had been touching both contacts at the same time. The twin result was a flash, a bang and a fried squirrel falling to the base of the pylon. Bearing a similar expression to that of the mouse!

# Chapter 6

## Charitable Fund Raising.

During my years at Yateley it continued to be a source of amazement and delight to me that the large majority of firefighters could and would find time to spend on fund raising for a variety of charities. All of us had full time jobs and most had families. Our local fire and rescue responsibilities could, at certain times of the year, be very time consuming. Yet regularly members of the station, often with help from family members, could be found running events like car washes, collections or sponsored wheelchair pushing. Even participating in events such as the annual British Heart Foundation London to Brighton bike ride, half marathons (well LFF Chris Sayers did) or triathlons.

I have an opinion that a significantly important factor encouraging these activities was that they all had confirmed positive outcomes which could go some way to counter some of the negative experiences we suffered during our work together.

There was also for us a very special local and significant need to be satisfied. Brian.

Brian is the severely handicapped son of LFF Danny Randall. I well remember the hugely difficult evening when Danny appeared on my doorstep with the good news that his wife Carolyn had delivered him a third son Brian. But that it was clear even from that early stage that the lad suffered physical disabilities and soon after his birth he was diagnosed with severe Cerebral Palsy. Brian became an important part of the station always welcome with his readiness to smile despite the continual pain and suffering he endures, especially if it is a joke at a firefighters expense. He is an inspiration to anyone who meets him. As too are Danny and Carolyn who at the same time have raised two other lads with all the normal demands that this makes upon any family, particularly during the teenage years.

We have been delighted to raise money to aid Brian's quality of life since the day he was born and were utterly amazed when, as part of our fund raising during our 25<sup>th</sup> Anniversary year, over £31,000, in various forms, was pulled together directly from our many initiatives in just twelve months.

Another focus for us as firefighters has been to collect for the National Firefighters Benevolent Fund. Many of the station members were regular contributors to this fundraising and many thousands of pounds were obtained by running car washes, sponsored events or holding straight forward collections, in particular just before Christmas at Blackbushe Sunday market

I cannot leave the subject of fund raising without making mention of a particular event we organised and to which our community's response was overwhelming.

Following the appalling scenes broadcast during and after the now infamous terrorist attacks in the United States on 9/11 many firefighters across the UK rallied to help the dependents of the 343 New York firefighters who were killed on that tragic day. We like so many other firefighters around the world saw it as our duty to do this.

At Yateley we organised a charity car wash at the station. People drove their cars into the station yard where we descended upon them, the cars that is, usually, with soap, water and sponge followed by a swift leathering off to produce sparkling results. Well more often than not! We had conducted car washes several times before and knew by experience that we should be able to raise a few hundred pounds for this cause. We were wrong. By the end of the day we had raised over £2000 pounds.

Throughout that day a long queue of cars patiently waited their turn whilst we soaped, sponged and leathered like never before. A particularly uplifting and often repeated occurrence was the number of people who just came to donate money. They would appear as if from nowhere, drop a £5 or £10 note into our collection buckets and be gone again without comment. It was a reflection of how the loss of life and circumstances around this event had deeply affected so many people in our community and they did not hesitate at the opportunity to show it.

# Chapter 7

## It's the Police!

We have always enjoyed a positive relationship with our local boys and girls in blue. Which was surprising when I stop to consider how unsupportive our actions may sometimes have seemed to them. A fresh, young, keen and eager new constable direct from training school always seemed fair game for us. Invariably he or she wanted to impress and we were only too pleased to help where we could. A particular way of helping we developed and used many times was at regular incidents involving car fires. The scenario would develop as follows.

Late at night we would get a call to a car fire. Invariably these cars had been stolen locally and used by joy riders or occasionally to support some other crime. These incidents were common. They were sometimes in an advanced state of destruction when we arrived because of the remote locality they were often found in and the delay between being set alight, someone discovering them and making a 999 call,.

Usually first in attendance we were followed very often by the local police in the form of a constable. Sometimes such constables were new to the area and so it could be our first time of meeting. Naturally we welcomed them and to show how helpful we could be supplied them with the registration number of the burnt out car. The registration, we told them, we just managed to note before the number plates burnt away.

This was very useful for them as they needed the registration to verify the vehicle ownership and in turn supply this to us as we needed the owner's details for the fire report we would have to complete. Pleased with the help they had received and keen to impress they would waste no time in returning to their car and proceed to radio their control for a vehicle check.

**Yateley Fire Station 2006**

**Yateley Fire Station 1980 -1985**
(Back) Sub O A Albury SC D Newman FF P Atkinson FF J Chivers FF N Gibson FF M West  FF M Bone
FF P Cook FF J Dean  FF A Fulcher FF J Bentley FF J Ashby FF C Rix
(Front) FF S Thomson FF W Robbins LFF  P Cullen Sub O C Ive LFF J Hicks FF D Randall FF C Cole

**Yateley Fire Station 2005**
(Back) FF A White  FF C Groves  FF S Geen  FF D Garwood  FF S Capp  FF N White
FF G Hyde  FF B Yarnall  FF P Cook  (Front) FF I Stones  FF R Pratley  LFF C Sayers
Sub O C Ive  LFF D Randall  FF K Blunt  FF D Buckland

Typical RTA involving car versus tree and as usual the tree wins!
Both the young male occupants survived.

**Community Fire Safety in action**
Presentation of smoke detectors to Newlands Primary School reception class

**New Years Eve 2001**
Three elderly people escape into water from car in flooded river.
Photo taken the following morning.

Hawley Auxiliary Firefighters with 'Robert' their first fire engine and
Scammel pump pictured outside Hawley House circa 1941

Yateley Auxiliary Firefighters with their first fire engine of donated Buick
car and Scammel pump pictured outside Yateley Drill Hall circa 1941

We observed them at a distance as their fresh keenness was transformed to acute embarrassment when they were informed over the radio, and with many other county police officers listening, that the owner of the vehicle was Hampshire Police. In fact it was the very car they were sitting in!

Being new the registration of their own patrol car was not something they thought much about, until then. We however had noted it as they had driven up.

**Difficult Situations**

As would be expected we did support each other where we could at incidents whether by teaming up with them to give CPR to a dying teenage girl victim of an RTA (one of the saddest and most tragic incidents I personally attended and of which I will write more later) or on one memorable occasion defusing what was about to develop into a violent situation with poor prospects for the officer concerned.

Returning from a call we turned into the road leading to the fire station and outside of the nearby police station. Here we were surprised to find the scene of six men confronting a single police officer in a very intimidating manner. Apparently other officers had just arrested their friend in what the men described as a "rough" manner. Two officers had bundled him into a car and driven off leaving the lone PC to try and placate the remaining crowd.

They were standing in the road and stopping us from returning to the fire station. A few of us descended from the pump and in a friendly way asked them to step aside. Confronted with a fire engine they seemed to instinctively do this, half to one side of the road and half to the other. With them separated the pump stopped between them, to pick us up again. But instead of remounting we carried on talking and listening sympathetically to their concerns. This action seemed to calm them down and remembering the drinks they had left on the bar in the adjacent pub they returned to them, leaving an untouched and grateful PC.

The neutrality of the fire service in this country is something we should be proud of and always seek to maintain. Should firefighters be attacked whilst conducting their duties it is a sure sign that law and order has broken down. Sadly this happened on two occasions during my time.

The first was when a family of travellers began to stone the crew and fire engine because we were putting out, what I considered to be because of its location, their dangerous bonfire. The police attended to assist us but by that time I had pulled us out to avoid a further deterioration of the situation. It was disappointing that on this occasion our senior fire brigade management chose not to pursue the matter and refused to prosecute.

That is not the end of the story for ironically just two weeks later this same group of travellers were in need of our services when one of their caravans caught alight. Naturally with the safety of my crew in mind I was very wary of attending this incident without adequate police and a senior brigade officer presence and organising this probably delayed our attendance and resulted in the van being a total write off. Such is life.

The second occasion we came under attack had a much more positive outcome. Whilst attending a rubbish fire on a certain local estate one of the firefighters was felled by a large piece of concrete thrown at him by someone in hiding. Again I withdrew the crew, summoned an ambulance to check him over and police and senior fire officers to investigate.

Although no serious injury was sustained and no arrests were subsequently made the incident seemed to have a significant affect on the local community. Meetings were organised by the local council, involving the residents, councillors, the housing association, police and ourselves. These became a regular occurrence focusing upon improving the quality of life for residents and others involved in the area. The positive result was that not only did no further incidents of this type take place but an estate to which we were called around 30 times per year suddenly dropped to zero calls over the following 14 months, adding considerably to the safety of that community!

A further example of how we cared for and supported our local Bobbies was how we liked to ensure that during a hot summer's day they remained cool. Soothing showers of cool, almost fresh, water would often be encountered by them when standing too close, in our opinion, to a fire we were busy extinguishing. Usually when they were least expecting it. The record was of five PC's and a Sergeant 'enjoying' this cool drenching at one time!

We may have been fortunate but over the years we have met many 'good coppers' who have endured our jokes with patience and seldom seeking revenge. Apart that is from one Christmas Eve when I popped into the reception area of the local 'Nick'.

Finding it unmanned as usual I gave several loud rings on the desk bell to summon them and dropped their Christmas card on the desktop as I left. I had barely returned to my car before being accosted by three burly coppers who delighted in spread eagling me over the bonnet of my car and proceeded to 'pat me down' in a search pattern, then behind a big smile which no one else could see and much finger wagging told me "Yes we know you have nothing wrong but the people watching don't." Sure enough the scene had attracted a number of onlookers and the impression being given was not good for my local reputation. I departed somewhat embarrassed knowing that it was no more than I deserved. Until we met again!

**My New Friend the American Traffic Cop**.

My personal experience of most significance in this relationship between firefighters and police officers occurred not in Yateley but thousands of miles from home in Flagstaff, Arizona, USA.

My wife Brenda and I were enjoying one of our first holidays without the kids, who were by now of an independent age. We were travelling out from Las Vegas enjoying the scenery of the state parks in this area. In no particular hurry but eager to make progress I must admit to have been breaking the speed limit by a few miles an hour whilst driving along a wide highway in a semi-urban area outside of the city of Flagstaff. The officer who suddenly appeared in his sheriff's car had a different view on this.

He appeared behind me out of the traffic and with blue lights flashing and siren wailing he made it very clear it was me he was after and expected me to pull over. Which I quickly did!

I decided to greet the officer rather than make him walk to the car and so stepped out to meet this rather large individual, equipped with regulation Hollywood mirrored sunglasses and hand firmly resting on his gun butt.

It was at this point I noticed the particular building we had stopped out side of. Adopting the ignorant tourist pose I greeted him in my broadest Queen's English accent and inquired of him what the trouble was. His southern drawl response was one of "The trouble for you is that you have just earned yourself a $480 fine for speeding at over 80 miles per hour!" Now as I said I admit to speeding but not at anywhere near this amount. Arguing with this somewhat intimidating individual did not seem the most appropriate action and, somewhat in desperation, I decided to take full advantage of my surroundings.

Maintaining my dumb British tourist pose I presented him with my UK driving licence which he had requested and additionally asked him if he would like to see some photo ID. These were the days prior to the UK photo ID driving licence. Responding to his grunted, "Sure would" as he was clearly baffled by the paper licence in his hand I presented him with my fire brigade ID card complete with photo. His attitude immediately became softer.

Taking off the glasses he asked, though clearly still suspicious, "So you're a firefighter?" "Yes" I responded with as friendly a smile as I could muster "Just like those guys over there" gesturing to the volunteer fire station we had stopped outside of. This did it. "Hey" he said, "You know these guys?" I replied I didn't but was looking forward to calling on them later that day.

He suddenly took a real interest in what I did and he clearly knew his local firefighters well. My final ace was to mention that I had attended the Windsor Castle fire. As with many Americans the royal family fascinated him and this broke down any remaining hostility as he wanted to know all about it.

Brenda was watching all of this intently through the adjusted rear view mirror but was unable to hear what was being said. She told me afterwards, but not before telling me off for speeding in the first place, that just by viewing the cop's body language it seemed I had gone from his public enemy number one to his best friend in a matter of a few minutes. She called me all sorts of names when I told her the whole story, she was right of course!

But I didn't get off scot free, not quite, just as we were about to part he apologised but said he still had to give me a ticket as it would be expected by his Captain who was the one who had clocked me on the radar gun. My heart sank; until he said it would be an $18 fine for 'wasting finite resources.' I accepted this with pleasure and trying to give an admonished look shook his hand warmly before driving off with Brenda's words of "You jammy git" ringing in my ears.

### An Unhappy Officer

I remember well one very irate copper who was upset one day when a simple incident occurred. This was not directly of our making but resulted in him having to account for damage to an expensive item of police equipment. It happened during one of the "Make a Wish" charity days we attended.

The Make a Wish charity provided special days out for children with life threatening illnesses. This event was held for several years until it outgrew the site on a 'Go Kart' race track at the rear of Blackbushe Airport. Many celebrities would attend and all sorts of vehicles would take the children for a ride around the track. These then parked up and allowed the children to climb over them.

We were there with the fire engine which as usual was proving very popular with the children. We always supervised the children as they sat behind the wheel encouraging their imagination to run free, but at an unguarded moment one young lady manage to release the handbrake. Not a major issue as we usually park on flat ground at such events in case this happens. But not this time!

It wasn't much of a slope and within a few seconds we had the handbrake back on after the machine had rolled back just a couple of feet. Unfortunately this was an inch or so too much as a police motorcyclist had decided to park his shiny new motor bike directly behind us. The rear of the fire engine barely touched the bike but this was sufficient to topple it over. This did not cause much damage to the bike however the officer had placed upon the saddle his new helmet, which contained within it expensive state of the art communications equipment. As the bike moved so the helmet rolled off of the saddle and the bike fell squarely upon it, doing, so we were informed, considerable damage to it! The officer was very upset and came to me seeking someone to blame. Although I sympathised with him the conversation finished when I suggested he looked in a mirror as it was he who parked the bike and placed the helmet in that position and no one else. A little harsh but we got away with it!

This charity event was always popular with us and we were keen to support such a worthy cause. It was clear that some of the children were very ill but perhaps the most touching memory for me was when I turned to help a young lad into the cab of the fire engine. He greeted me with a look of concern and the comment "It's alright Mister, it's not me who's dying it's my brother!" as he pointed to a bald younger brother who was clearly undergoing chemotherapy treatment.

As I mentioned celebrities would often attend and on one occasion the Formula One racing driver David Coulthard appeared. He came over showed a keen interest in our fire engine and LFF John Hicks in turn took a keen interest in him. John was something of a "Piston Head" and could spend hours and hours, and hours talking about cars. If you let him! John showed him over the pump and David told us that as a young lad growing up he had always wanted to be a fireman. I said it was funny how things worked out as John had always wanted to be a Formula One racing driver!

There was one other occasion when our local boys in blue were not that impressed with our activities. It was the occasion of one of the firefighter's stag night. The lucky man, accompanied by many members of the station, had visited a number of local drinking establishments and by the end of the evening was unsteady on his legs. In fact he couldn't stand up.

Being ever resourceful the lads commandeered a shopping trolley from a local supermarket to convey him back to the station in. It was as they were doing this that they were spotted by "Big Nigel", as we affectionately referred to this local Bobbie, cruising the area in his patrol car. On seeing a bunch of men behaving suspiciously with a shopping trolley he anticipated an open and shut case. Then pulling up he recognised the guys and following a greeting of "Oh no not you lot!" he gave them a rollicking and told them to make sure the trolley was returned, which I am reliably assured it was.

We celebrated a number of the firefighters' marriages in this way including another who at the end of his stag night found himself manacled around a lamp post and inspected by two passing WPC's.

However he believed himself more fortunate than another member who had strange patterns painted over his naked body. Luckily he was not inspected by two passing WPC's! All finished the night sober. This was assured as they were tied to a ladder and hosed down with copious supplies of cold water. Importantly all had very successful weddings.

I cannot leave this chapter without giving mention by name to some of the highly respected officers we encountered. PC's such as a local legend Mick Hayden, Andy Grieve, Mark Sayers and Keith Burridge. A multitude of WPC's and in particular the two very short individuals who upon appearing from a dark wood together late one night were greeted with "Have you Hobbits walked over from the Shire?" and thus from then on were known to us as 'them Hobbits'.

Lastly I must mention Sergeant Chris Corby a man full of wit who commenced the speech at his retirement function by referring to his dear old mum and dad, apparently his dad fell ill and his caring mother rubbed the old man's chest with goose fat, he went down hill pretty quick after that! Such was the humour of the man. Humour that is hugely welcome in what would otherwise be a very sterile world indeed.

# Chapter 8

## A Military Dimension

Much of the fire ground we were responsible for was owned by the Ministry of Defence and regularly used by the army. As a result encounters with them or their ordnance were common place and on one occasion resulted in a nasty injury to a member of our crew.

As we carried out our fire fighting duties we often stumbled across soldiers in camouflage armed to the teeth with all sorts of weaponry. Fortunately the area was not used for live firing and we were regularly assured, by those soldiers, that the loud popping noises occurring as fire swept across the grass was simply the noise given off by blank cartridges dropped by a trainee squaddie during some war game. Assured but we were never really convinced. Although the fact that none of us ever suffered any wound from these must have proven this to be the case. Or we were just very, very, lucky!

A blank cartridge did cause one injury however which I fully admit would not have occurred had I kept my hands in my pocket!

One summer's day we had finished knocking down the flames of a not particularly large grass fire and I sent the pump off to replenish with water from the nearest hydrant. Waiting for its return the devil found work for idle hands, mine!

Those of us left sat with beaters watching the smouldering embers still waiting to be doused ensuring that a sudden gust of wind did not suddenly transformed them into flames and undo the good work already completed.

I couldn't help picking up a spent cartridge and noticing Danny standing a short way away I tossed it at him. I remember watching as it arced through the air and went cold as it struck him just above the left eye. I was horrified and he was both cut and livid. Though as I remember more livid than cut! I was continually punished for quite a while after as Danny made sure that all of the crew knew how I'd assaulted him.

I think this was the one occasion when I managed to dig deep enough and found some sympathy for him, but not a lot or he might have thought I cared!

Being geographically located close to the home of the British Army with several military locations within our fire ground we have attended numerous incidents on their land, normally these have been trouble free but occasionally their weaponry caused us some real stress

During the IRA campaign of bombings in England security at the local army bases was at its height. Armed sentries with live ammunition loaded and ready for use patrolled and staffed the gates.

One morning we received a call to an aircraft which had crashed onto the sports field of a local barracks. Attending we were met by a nervous young man armed with a rifle and ready for anything. He told us he was there to escort us to the scene of the incident so could he get on board.

Security or not there was no way I was going to have someone armed with a loaded weapon on my fire engine, especially this spotty faced adolescent and I told him so. Fortunately a sergeant quickly appeared and on learning of the situation he readily agreed to be our unarmed escort. Journeying through the camp to the crash site it was clear to see it was on a high state of alert and on arrival we could not help but notice the numerous young men deployed around the field laying prone in firing position with rifles seemingly pointing our way. "Don't worry about them," the sergeant said, "You're quite safe so long as you are with me."

Needless to say we stayed very close to our new friend for the entire time of the incident. As it transpired the aircraft had not crashed but had run out of fuel several hundred metres short of the runway of a nearby airfield and had made a forced landing onto the nearest flat green space the pilot could see. He was happy to be down but the camp anticipating this aircraft dropping out of the sky on them could be the start of a terrorist raid had gone to full alert and deployed the troops. All ended well but we were not happy until well out of the line of fire.

Much of this army training area is wooded and the ground in many parts consists of layers of peat in some places over a foot in depth. Subsequently in wet, or normal summer conditions, this peat becomes laden with water and helps to reduce the risk of and damp down any fires. In dry and particularly drought conditions the reverse is true and a fire is able to find its way down into the dry fibrous peat. This will then quite happily burn away underground for weeks on end slowly spreading out from its original centre then, if left undisturbed, readily spring up from below igniting any dry grass or bracken it encounters. In doing so creating more work for the hapless firefighter! It is important during such weather conditions we locate even the smallest fire as quickly as possible and treat it to copious supplies of water, quite literally cutting into the peat with our high pressure jets of water.

It was on a call during such conditions that we come to the story of the firefighter who made the mistake of admitting to us for the first time of a phobia he suffered from. The incident commenced with a call to what was described as a small fire burning in the peat deep in the woods. With the lightly rapidly failing I was keen that we found and dealt with the fire as quickly as possible. It was rough ground for walking around on in the darkness and peppered with slit trenches dug by the military during their manoeuvres.

After locating the general area described by the caller and leaving the pump and driver at the edge of the wood the crew and myself set off into the growing gloom to search for the burning peat. As we spread out we searched across a growing area so maintaining contact with each other became more difficult. It was at this point that our colleague chirped up with the information, until then totally unknown by the rest of us, that he was afraid of the dark and had no torch! It was a simple thing really and to many a perfectly rational phobia. As the reader may have already observed from previous pages, firefighters have a wicked and often merciless sense of humour and will exploit any personal perceived or real weakness of a colleague.

Little response was made following his announcement but as we spread out into the wood it was as if by following some telepathic inclination the rest of the crew seemed to melt away into the darkness leaving him feeling very much alone. Indeed his plaintive cry of "Oi you bastards" initially drew no response from his hidden crew mates. Eventually and moved by the whimpering we recovered our erstwhile friend who once reunited with us repeated his curses but admitted that like many before him, and since, he had learned the lesson that having a weakness is perfectly acceptable. So long as you don't tell anyone about it!

Possibly the unkindest example of this was the firefighter who let it be known that he had a dread of snakes. Subsequently there was many a time when damping down embers after a common fire was in progress that he would look up in response to his name being called to see a snake arcing though the air towards him tossed by one of his crew 'mates'! Quite dead having succumbed to its fate during the fire, but he didn't know that!

The army training area was a regular location for fires caused either by army pyrotechnics or local youngsters committing lighters or matches to mischief.

# Chapter 9

## Fires & Rescues

An enduring image the public have of firefighters rescuing people from burning buildings is a popular one but I am pleased to say not one which occurs very often. We should much prefer that there was never a fire in the first place or if there was that everyone had escaped safely before we arrived. There were though times when we did indeed encounter this challenge and on such occasions the benefit of the constant training we had undertaken and the team work we had developed was key to its repeated successful outcome.

### Naked Support

Our first live rescue was memorable for being just that. This happened in the first few months of the station becoming operational and in many ways finally proved to a few remaining sceptics of senior officer rank within Hampshire Fire Brigade that we had developed into a fully operational and experienced unit.

The call was to a "Persons Reported" in a house in Blackwater. Persons Reported means that the 999 caller believes there is a person or people trapped in a fire. These calls, though fortunately few and far between, call for a very swift response and a high state of readiness on arrival.

As the crew pulled up smoke could be clearly seen coming from the premises. FF Danny Randall and FF Chris Rix were smartly in the door wearing BA and quickly began a room by room search of the house. In a bedroom they found an unconscious woman. She was stark naked. This did not slow down our intrepid firefighters. Danny grabbed her legs and Chris the area in front of her chest! They soon had her out into the open air. Explaining his rescue technique later Chris insisted that the only good hold he could get to carry her out was by having a firm, and full, hand on each side. Sounded plausible to us! I understand that the lady in question made a full recovery.

A short while later an officer turned up to congratulate the crew on their rescue and the Chief Fire Officer sent his own congratulations via the teleprinter. Such small messages can have an excellent effect on morale.

**Not Dying Tonight!**

Our next rescue was far more complicated if not a little bizarre. We were called to a house on fire in Yateley and arrived to find smoke coming out of a kitchen door. I committed our standard approach to such an incident which resulted in 2 BA wearers equipped with a high pressure hose reel charged with water going through the open door of the kitchen. Here they extinguished a curious set of small fires involving towels and paper scattered around the room.

This immediately indicated to us that we had a likely arson on our hands and I passed this information on to the police who had just arrived. In return they informed me that the lady occupier of the house was well known to them and had unpredictable behaviour based on her drug habit. But she was nowhere to be seen. As the smoke in the kitchen cleared I stood the BA crew down and started to take a look around the house.

As I climbed the stairs I realised there was a curtain of smoke building up on the first floor landing. This appeared to be coming from a further fire which, looking under the smoke curtain, I could see was coming from a bedroom to the right of where I stood. I recalled the BA team to come up and deal with it.

Turning to make my way back down I noticed a light coming from a bedroom to my left and the door slightly ajar. Smoke can cause serious damage to property and so I decided to close the door before leaving. As I reached it I was startled to see through the opening a woman standing on the other side of the room from where I stood. This was not something I was expecting and the surprise of it nearly made me jump out of my skin!

"What are you doing?" I asked and at first she just gazed at me before replying "Leave me alone I'm going to die!" She seemed almost hysterical but as she was only armed with a lipstick, which she seemed to be waving at me in a threatening way. A fact that registered clearly with me at the time as farcical. I replied "No you're not!" and threw her over my shoulder in the standard fireman's carry, which I had performed in training many times but this was the one and only time I was to perform it for real .

Gripping her tightly I was soon on my way back down the stairs meeting on the way FF Chris Parker who was one of the BA team on their way up. I remember clearly Chris's eye's growing as large as saucers as we moved passed him and out on to the street, he was as surprised as me!

Upon putting the lady down created another challenge. She just wanted to get back into the house so determined was she to complete her suicide and she did not take kindly, from the language she used, to us sitting on her to prevent this.

The police then appeared and took over with an even firmer hand. Back in the house the BA crew had quickly dealt with the fire in the bedroom. Checking out the other rooms they found a partially completed suicide note in lipstick scrawled across the wall of the room I had found the lady in. The reason for her holding the lipstick when I discovered her!

All in all it was a strange call. Although we tried hard at all of the incidents we attended we know we did not always make everyone happy. But this was the first time someone had demonstrated their dissatisfaction by trying to run back into the fire!

**"I Knew You'd Come!"**

As more experience was gained so certain calls became routine, even boring. Often the dullest of these were calls to Automatic Fire Alarms or AFA's as we knew them.

Automatic Alarm Systems are fitted in numerous establishments from Factories to Offices to Hospitals and Nursing homes. Make no mistake the principle of these systems is sound. In simple terms smoke or heat detectors are strategically placed throughout a building and electronically connected to a central alarm panel. This in turn is commonly linked to a remote central monitoring station staffed twenty four hours a day. When a detector head operates the control panel sends notice of an alarm to the monitoring station. Staff there notify the fire brigade responsible for the area the premises are located in and a suitable prearranged attendance of fire appliances is despatched to deal with the incident.

The problem with such systems was that any number of reasons from electrical storms, faulty equipment or software to insects or burnt toast could trigger a detector head to operate. Such incorrect operation of the system created a false alarm.

These false alarms have been common place in some areas and particularly those for fire stations serving sizeable towns. For example there was a period in the 1990's when over 40% of calls responded to by Basingstoke Fire Station in Hampshire were recorded as false alarms from AFA systems. A clear waste of resource and demotivator for all those concerned!

At Yateley we were fortunate the number of these calls were for us comparatively low. Whenever one's pager sounded it was not until attending the station that the reason for its operating became available via the teleprinter readout. As a result one was always focused whilst responding to the station upon the possibility that the call could be to a situation which tested your knowledge, fitness and fire and rescue

94

capabilities. When one saw on the readout sheet that the call was to an AFA and due to the amount of times these resulted in a false alarm deflation and routine set in and the urgency of attending could become lost.

Fortunately it was because of the routine of grabbing kit and getting the pump out of the door which ensured the urgency remained, and this was certainly important in one of my most memorable calls.

It was 10:20 hrs on 29th March 2005. Responding to our pagers we arrived at the station to find that we were being sent over the county border into Berkshire as the second attending appliance to an AFA at an elderly persons' residence made up of independent flats. It was a place we knew well. We had attended false alarms there a number of times before along with our colleagues from Crowthorne fire station, in whose fire ground the premises were located.

Halfway there a sudden radio message completely changed the nature of the incident and our attitude towards it. The message was that a call had been received directly from the premises informing fire brigade control that someone was trapped in a flat where a fire was in progress. Thus the incident become one of 'persons reported.'

Such information is guaranteed to sharpen any firefighters reactions. A few quick words from me and BA was donned and all crew members knew their tasks. As expected when we arrived the Crowthorne pump was already there and members of their crew had entered the building to locate the affected flat.

Leaving my crew at full readiness outside I ventured in to liaise with the Leading Firefighter in charge. I found him and two of his crew, rigged in BA, just as they had located the flat. Sure enough smoke was percolating from around its locked door indicating that indeed a severe fire was in progress on the other side.

Suddenly a Carer attending some of the residents appeared. She told us that a Mrs Doris Smith was certainly in the flat and that she was 102 years old. I recall my first thought at this news was that judging by the smoke Doris would be extremely fortunate to get much older! The good news was that the Carer had a key.

With the Crowthorne firefighters starting up their BA I took the key and unlocked the door. As I did so I noticed that despite the clear indications of fire the door itself was cold to the touch. This indicated that the fire was not close to the door. As the BA team finalised their preparations, and keeping low so as to allow the smoke to travel safely above me, I opened the door to speed up their entry. As it opened I could see that the area of the flat immediately in front of me was full of a thick dense, and by its chemical construction, toxic smoke. Then as I peered into this hell I could see something else, something which appeared orange and woolly!

My immediate thought was this was a garment hanging on a clothes airer. Still keeping low I reached forward, touched it and quickly learned the truth of what I had found. It was a garment alright and Doris was in it! She was standing up in the smoke with her back to me and, so I later learnt, holding on to her walking frame.

Without hesitation I grabbed her around the waist and pulled her out and away from the now billowing clouds of smoke pouring from the room, dragging her into the corridor just as the BA team passed us on their way in to fight the fire.

Carrying her along the corridor away from the smoke I met FF Ian Stones from our crew and our most highly medically trained member. He quickly had an oxygen mask on Doris and I recall being simply staggered that although shocked and confused she was conscious and able to talk to us. She was taken off to hospital where after just a short stay  was released fully fit!

The fire was subsequently found to have been caused by an electrical fault in a bathroom extractor fan. Being made primarily of plastic this generated the large amount of toxic smoke.

Several months later I returned to visit Doris in her repaired and redecorated flat. She was well and we were both pleased to see each other. I asked her why she was where she was when I found her. She replied "I was aware there was a fire but I knew that so long as I stood holding on to my frame I'd be ok. I knew you'd come and find me!" A remarkable and very fortunate lady whom I am pleased to say enjoyed several more years of life following her very narrow escape.

**Perfect CPR - tragic loss.**

Over the years Yateley firefighters have attended many types of incidents from tragedy to comedy. As a result almost all of us have sad images forever in our memories. None sadder than those involving young people who have lost their lives as a result of a road traffic accident.

In the late evening of June 18th 1993 we received a call to an RTA persons trapped on the Yateley/Eversley border. As soon as we were in attendance we found that although no one was trapped we were dealing with a challenging and, despite all of our endeavours, tragic incident.

Two teenagers walking back from work at a local pub had been struck from behind by a car. One was a girl of sixteen and the other a boy of seventeen. LFF John Hicks and I went to assist a young policeman who was busy performing CPR on the girl. The remainder of the crew set to work securing the safety of the scene from other traffic with cones, signs and flashing blue lights and then helping with the young man.

As we took over from the policeman an ambulance arrived and after a quick assessment they connected her to a heart monitor and left us to carry on whilst they dedicated their time to the lad. As we worked we could see the graph projected on to the monitor's screen that the life signs looked good and encouraged by this we worked on.

A short while later an Immediate Care scheme doctor appeared on the scene. These doctors are GPs available to respond to emergencies in their local areas who have voluntarily undertaken specialist training in dealing with accident victims, or severe trauma cases as they call them. We met on numerous times over the years and were very thankful for their expertise. Although on this occasion he turned our hope to a sad acceptance of the situation before us.

As was normal practice we quickly appraised him of the situation and what we had been doing pointing out as we worked the positive responses on the monitor. Instructing us to stop he quickly examined the still body before us. Sadly he shook his head and said "Sorry gentlemen but I'm afraid she's gone." Vainly protesting we pointed at the monitor, though now showing a flat line. "That just showed you were performing the CPR correctly." he added and turned away to assist the ambulance staff with their business.

John and I were devastated and although we carried on with our duties helping with the young man who was seriously injured and clearing up the scene it was a difficult few hours for the whole crew.

A personal twist to this incident for me was that the police identified the lad as the son of some very old friends of mine whom I have known since we were teenagers together, well before either of us had moved to Yateley. I am pleased to close this particular story by reporting that although it took a while he made a good recovery.

Over the years we attended a large number of RTA's which resulted in fatalities. Many of these were as a result of speed or drink or more often than not a mixture of both. I do not intend to relate many more of these stories out of respect for the feelings of the families of these victims. Nor for the risk of rekindling the unpleasant memories which all firefighters retain no matter how much time passes and are never really forgotten.

We were fortunate never to have had to attend an accident which resulted in the death or serious injury of one of our family members. Sadly this is an occasional experience suffered by retained firefighters throughout the country. By the nature of the local area to their home where they provide fire and rescue cover the situations of firefighters attending an RTA where a close family member, son, daughter, father etc has been the victim does sadly happen. For me the experience of identifying the body of a young man whom I knew and was in the same school year as my eldest son was more than enough to have to cope with.

None of us are super human and we are subject to suffering from the grief that fatal incidents can inflict. In recent years the fire service set up counselling services to assist anyone with such a problem and they ensure that the availability of this service is well known to all firefighters.

From my own experience our closeness as a team and our ability to talk about the situations we encountered enabled most issues to be resolved. On return to station from a fatal or particularly traumatic incident we would sit down there and then and discuss our feelings with each other. We would then follow this up with a detailed analysis of the call to the remainder of the station on the following drill night again bringing out how we felt.

It was important that all of us understood that it was ok to show one's feelings, and we did. Certainly though it could be tough at times.

## Air Crash December 23rd 2000

A tragic incident which was for me yet another of the most memorable during my years of fire fighting occurred on the overcast misty dank day of December 23rd 2000.

99

The time was 14:00 hrs. I was sitting at my home PC trying to work on a dissertation for the Masters in Business Administration degree I was undertaking at that time. For this paper I had set out to analyse the team working of a crew of retained firefighters at an incident against that of a team of engineers working on an R & D project.

This latter area I had fully in hand using a team of engineers from Nokia the company that was my employer at that time. The fire fighting team however was giving me a problem as the material I needed to analyse could only come from a crew dealing with a significant incident and one had not occurred in our area for some time. I was contemplating whether in light of this to change my approach entirely when my pager sounded and things dramatically changed.

Arriving at the fire station a minute or so later the information provided by the teleprinter immediately indicated that this call would not be a routine one. The incident was described as "Light aircraft landed on factory". For some reason this gave me the image of a single engine aircraft, of which there were many flying regularly at nearby Blackbushe airfield, resting more or less intact upon the factory roof.

The factory, which manufactured a range of rubber products, was well known to us as we had from time to time attended AFA's due to a faulty fire detection system on the premises. During these incidents we had taken advantage of the opportunity to walk around the factory and its associated offices and found it occupied by a company who had safety very much at the front of the working processes. This was demonstrated by the numerous safety signs around the walls and general tidiness of the factory floor and office areas, together with a high standard of fire protection systems, more of which I shall describe later. Ironic then that it should be the scene of such a devastating incident involving multiple loss of life which literally exploded upon it.

As we made our way to the incident I was informed by our fire control that multiple 999 calls had been received to an aircraft crashed into the factory. We had learned over the years that when such multiple calls are received it is a clear indication that a significant incident was in progress. We mentally prepared ourselves for this.

Heading towards the incident it was impossible to observe any early indications of a fire as the low cloud and dull wet conditions prevented us detecting any tell tale column of smoke. Until that is we entered the industrial estate where the factory was located. Here we noticed bystanders pointing the way into the mist. Then around just 100 metres from the site a blossom of orange flame pierced out of the gloom and we were rapidly confronted with a serious fire. This was enveloping around a third of the factory building and, ominously, there were no obvious signs of the remains of any aircraft.

Here I quote directly from the report I wrote on the evening of the incident.

"On arriving at the scene I was confronted as I faced the building with a severe fire approximately 10 metres inside it. This could be easily viewed through the large hole to ground level in the side wall of the building immediately facing me. I also noticed a broken down fence and debris scattered across an adjacent grass verge and road immediately in front of the building and to the left of my position.

At this point I became aware that the Blackbushe Airport fire appliance was also in attendance and getting a jet to work with 2BA wearers. I instructed two of my crew to also start up their BA sets and the others to lay out a main jet for them to work with. I then sent an informative message describing what was happening and requested an additional six pumps to assist in dealing with the incident.

Upon alighting from the pump I called to the airport firefighters not to enter the building further than they had, approximately 6 metres, as I was concerned about building collapse. A Blackbushe Airport firefighter approached me for instructions and I asked him to check the rear of the building for any sign of fire. In my immediate appraisal of the incident I decided that the chance of survivors was small but moved to the left of the scene to survey the factory yard.

I noticed two large shutter doors, one each on the remaining two thirds of the building, which extended to its full height. Both appeared to be bowed outwards and off their 'runners'. This indicated to me that an explosion had taken place inside the building, which I assumed to have occurred during the aircraft impact. I entered briefly through one of these doors to check for internal fire spread but quickly saw that the internal fire shutters had operated and no fire was present.

I returned to my pump to check fire-fighting operations and on walking to the right of the building I noticed a bulge in the sidewall about half way along, which again I took as being caused by the explosion on impact. A great deal of water was running out of the building carrying on it aviation fuel and I noticed that the sprinkler system within the factory was activated in the area of the fire.

Although the indications were that no one could have survived the impact I used those of us available to undertake a casualty search of the area both inside and outside of the building. But to no avail. Other pumps then started to arrive taking care of the rear of the building, providing further BA support and dealing with the run off of water to prevent it entering nearby drains."

Whilst all of this was happening a police presence was also building up and they set up an exclusion zone to complement the safety zone we had taped off in the immediate vicinity of the building. This proved very useful in controlling the media who materialised within minutes of our attendance. Apparently they, including BBC and ITN news teams, had been on their way to cover a fox hunting event which was due to take place nearby that afternoon and as the newswires picked up reports of our incident so they were diverted to it.

It was not long before the BA teams found the sad remains of the five people reported to be on the aircraft at take off. Apparently they had intended to celebrate Christmas together in Spain. This was confirmed after the fires were beaten down and further searching of the debris revealed the macabre finding of a turkey sat amongst the smouldering wreckage singed brown as though it had been taken straight from the oven!

This incident though certainly tragic in its consequences with the destruction and loss of human life was ironically from the perspective of fire fighting and fire protection successful. The rapid deployment coupled with the hard work of the fire fighting team restricted the fire to the initial area of the impact.

Two positive events also aided this. Firstly the initiative of the airport fire crew to attend. Normally they restrict their operations to within the perimeters of the airfield. Secondly the location, just feet from our pump, of a hydrant. Deploying jets to work as we did results in the very rapid use of the 2000 litres of water carried on the fire engine so locating and setting into a street hydrant is always high on the agenda for any pump operator. As LFF John Hicks, our driver that day, quite rightly reminded me. To park adjacent to one as we did on this occasion was a piece of real good fortune.

Further important aids for us were the fire protection measures of the factory. As previously mentioned the factory owners gave safety a very high priority for both their staff and their premises. As a result there was a water sprinkler system fitted throughout the building and large steel fire shutters which once a fire was detected dropped down and compartmentalised the factory. When the aircraft exploded the steel shutters dropped and ensured that the fire could not spread to areas where the flammable rubber compounds were stored. Additionally the explosion caused 35 sprinkler heads to operate in the area of the fire adding to the deluge of water from the firefighters hoses and significantly aiding their work.

The only negative issue outside the tragedy of the incident was one which we experienced the next day when we returned to assist a police team in the recovery of the bodies. Always a difficult task and not one made any easier by the sudden flash which betrayed the presence inside the police cordon of a hidden press photographer as we carried a set of remains to the ambulance. Such appalling behaviour is experienced only too often by emergency services and is the very worst of media intrusion. He was quickly ushered away by the police but this lust for news and photographs by the British press at almost any price does little for respecting the victims or their families and impinges upon the dignity which should be afforded to them at such times.

**Blazing Stables**

As previously described incidents dealing with animals were often eventful and some times very challenging. Probably the best example of this was the call we received in November of 1993 to a fire at a riding stables.

The stables were located in Eversley in a lane that led at one end to the nearby river Blackwater and at the other out to the major road of the A327 and several miles on in turn to the A30. It was a quiet leafy lane which on that sunny afternoon was dramatically turned into a scene of fire, smoke, destruction, panicking horses and some very frightened people.

Responding in our usual fashion we were quickly mobile to the incident. Very soon after the pump had left the station we could see from the cab a smoke plume in the area of our destination that confirmed there was a fire and it seemed a significant one at that.

As we entered the lane in which the stables were located a further indicator of the seriousness of the incident became very apparent. Horses were running in a clear panic towards us, first one then in twos and threes until we had to take drastic avoiding action. Clearly there was a serious situation awaiting us.

As we turned the final corner to the stables entrance it became clear that a substantial blaze had taken hold in a long row of stalls. Confirming our attendance via radio with our control I requested a third pump to be sent and also warned the second pump, which I knew to be well on its way, of the marauding and terrified horses they would encounter on the roads as they travelled closer to the fire scene. As indeed they did.

One or two horses were still loose in the stable yard but the gate was wide open and we were able to drive straight in and pull up alongside the blazing stalls. Quickly getting jets to work we were aware that the nearest hydrant was some way away but that we were close to a river and this would indeed prove to be our best source of water.

As the jets began to work so the flames were quickly knocked down. It was then we saw for the first time the sad sight of the remains of two horses which being unable to escape had been engulfed by the smoke and flame and died in their stalls. We were able to successfully prevent the fire from reaching other areas of the establishment including the indoor riding arena.

The flames were soon extinguished and damping down operations commenced with the welcome assistance of the second and third pumps, the last of which set a portable pump into the river and laid hose to provide us with replenishment of the water our jets had so greedily sucked from our tank.

For me it was time to take stock and turn my attention away from the fire fighting operations to that of helping the fire investigation officer, sent by our fire control, to establish what caused the fire in the first place.

105

We commenced this work by seeking out witnesses in the form of those who initially discovered the fire and so called us out. I quickly came across several very distressed young ladies who worked at the premises as stable girls. It was they who had discovered the fire and released the horses from their stalls. Doing this they found the stable yard filled quickly with horses milling about clearly terrified of the fire around them. To relieve this situation the girls had only one option, to open the main gate of the stables and allow them to escape into the surrounding area, including inevitably the local road system which explained the horses we and the other pumps had encountered on our journeys.

The girls were clearly upset and became more so as news began to arrive, via the police, of the fate of some of the released horses. Almost thirty horses had been released. But tragically three of these had to be destroyed following collisions with vehicles on the open road. Although fortunately no people were injured!

The girls were grief stricken at the loss of these animals for which they had responsibility and immediately began to blame themselves for their deaths. But, as I firmly and repeatedly pointed out, had they not opened the gate I upon our arrival would most certainly have done so. It would have been impossible to have fought the fire from the road and from the aspect of ensuring the safety of my firefighters I would have had no option, nor hesitation, in releasing these animals. As I again repeatedly told them the action they took in releasing the poor creatures from their stalls undoubtedly saved their lives. Even with the loss out on the highway over twenty five horses were safe and that was the most significant fact for them to hold on to.

A footnote to this incident reflected once again the negative reporting of our press. The following week the local paper concentrated almost entirely on the loss of the horses on the road. Giving hardly any mention to the truly heroic acts the girls had performed to save the lives of so many others. This negative reporting did little for the credibility of the press but without doubt added to the shock and pain the girls would suffer for many weeks to come.

I cannot leave this story without reference to an incident which provided some light relief for us and as usual an element of embarrassment for one of our number.

During the damping down operations lines of hose with branches attached had been laid out and only when we were certain that all embers had been fully extinguished did we commence the task of 'making up'. One of these lines of hose had been taken into the indoor riding school and this was the one which LFF Danny Randall chose to clear away.

Once there is no longer any need for the pump it is turned off but the water still in the hose remains under the pressure generated by the pump until the hose branch is opened. This particular hose line had somehow been subjected to a considerable level of pressure so held within it water just waiting for the opportunity to gush out at high velocity. Danny provided that opportunity with hilarious results!

As Danny turned the lever to open the branch the built up pressure was so great it lifted him off of his feet. But ever the dedicated fire fighter he held grimly on knowing that had he let go the flailing branch could have done him a serious injury. As he held tight to the branch he pushed all of his weight on it to keep it, and him, close to the ground. So successful was he in doing this that the water jet speared into the floor of the arena throwing up a great shower of wood shavings held together with a mixture of general dirt, dung and, so it seemed to those watching, all sorts of nasty sticky substances. Substances which rapidly caked our intrepid firefighter and leaving him, as the pressure quickly decreased, standing a forlorn figure covered from head to toe in 'it'!

I remember quite clearly how those of us present at the time would have been only too willing to rush forward and help had we not a) determined it was a time for self preservation rather than valour. b) been able to stand up for the sight of poor Danny covered as he was in, let's call it a whole lot of "poo", had us doubled up with laughter. We managed to pull ourselves together and being the good friends that we were took great delight in hosing Danny down with copious supplies of fresh clean water. Well it was either that or he would have had to have walked home!

**The TV Effect**

The strong influence of television upon our lives today is responsible for moulding many of our perceptions of life and our expectations of what will happen should we ever be confronted with a dangerous or threatening situation. Such situations involving fire or the threat of fire are commonly portrayed on the screen but more often than not bear little resemblance to reality. As a result we have seen both an over and under reaction by ordinary people when confronted by the reality of such an emergency.

We experienced a number of examples of this over the years but perhaps the best place to start is our involvement in providing fire cover for a TV programme being shot on location at the rear of Blackbushe Airport.

The series made and shown in the late eighties was entitled "Dempsey & Makepeace". The episode we were providing cover for was the first in the series and one which obviously needed, from the production companies perspective, to go with a bang. Our job was to take care of any incident resulting from the effects of too big a bang!

The storyline was the crash of a large lorry which, in the final cut, appeared to be travelling along a road when it hit a bump and turned over careering along on its side until exploding in a ball of smoke and flame. All very impressive but a piece which took around two days for the film company to get the effect they wanted for the show.

The first part of the filming was, to us, relatively easy. Using one of the now redundant second world war runways of the airfield to imitate a road

108

a stunt driver drove the lorry on to a ramp, hidden from the cameras, which flipped it over, whilst he jumped out. The vehicle then slid along for a while on its side until coming to rest on the grass by the side of the runway.

Fairly impressive but not that spectacular, then the special effects department began their work. They spent the next 5 hours or so adding incendiary and explosive devices to the lorry which once set off was expected to create the desired devastating effect. Whilst this was going on we amused ourselves by assisting and helped to add as much fuel to the fire as we could from the supplies provided by the film crew.

During this time a sudden shower of rain started and we ran for the shelter of our cab. At the same time inviting the eye catching star of the show, Glynis Barber who played the lead role of Makepeace, to come in out of the rain and sit in the back of the fire engine with us. Somewhat unsurprisingly she smiled but politely refused. She had obviously heard about a certain firefighter's problem with flatulence!

The rain stopped and after several more hours all was ready for the big bang. The safety area was cleared of all people and we sat back as the cameras began to roll and the order of "Action" was given. A few seconds later and the lorry was detonated with a resulting spectacular ball of flame and accompanying explosion. We looked on and were thoroughly enjoying the show when someone noticed that the explosion had set fire to the surrounding grass and a real drama was possibly about to unfold.

Quickly remembering that this was in fact the reason we were there we sped into action and had the outbreak extinguished in no time. To us this appeared to be a successful take which gave the effect the film company was seeking to create. But apparently not! After viewing rushes of the days filming the producers were not satisfied with the explosion and wanted one even more spectacular than the first so the next day they repacked the lorry with even more explosive and pyrotechnics than the day before and blew it up all over again!

The scene of the lorry turning over and exploding took just a few seconds to broadcast as early scenes in the opening episode but in reality had taken a huge amount of special effects and two days of time to create.

A negative effect of this type of creative fiction is that it is commonly believed by the general public to be of total fact and so in turn when confronted by a possibly dangerous situation people can act illogically to the danger confronting them. This can create more problems for the emergency services to deal with.

Perhaps the clearest examples I can give of such illogical fiction based behaviour, but importantly to the person concerned at the time perfectly logical, are as follows:

We were called to a routine, for us, car fire one day. It was in daytime and a car travelling along a local road had stopped after an electrical fault caused a fire in the engine compartment. As we arrived we could see a gentlemen, the owner of the vehicle, running round and round it. He was shouting at the top of his voice "Look out it's gonna blow!" over and over again. His panic was spreading to other bystanders who were seen running for cover. He seemed somewhat bemused by us positioning the fire engine relatively close, but not of course too close, to the fire. The flames had certainly taken hold of the vehicle spreading into the saloon compartment and greedily consuming the fuel provided by the plastic fascias and seats they found there.

We set to work knocking down these flames with our two hose reels and quickly had the situation fully under control, with a thankful but saddened motorist surveying the scene of destruction of his once pride and joy.

The expectation that a burning car will always explode into a dramatic ball of flame is a myth. One generated by television programmes and films as I described above. We are living proof that this just does not happen to any ordinary car, unless packed with some significant explosive or incendiary devices. But unless it's planned to be used for a terrorist attack this is not likely. It's true that loud bangs and pops will be heard when a car is burning and it is sensible to move a safe distance away from the fire and out of the toxic smoke it generates.

We treated all incidents with respect. But over 25 years we have attended hundreds of car fires and never encountered an exploding petrol tank. We have had one or two split which can cause a small but spectacular running fuel fire. I recall one particular occasion when this happened. Burning fuel spread quickly across the road and under a Surrey fire engine which had stopped downhill of the burning vehicle. Much I must admit to our amusement.

Such fires are easily handled with our standard equipment and fire fighting techniques. The bangs heard are often the tyres exploding. It's a common occurrence during a car fire but produces nothing more than a need for any firefighter standing next to one when it goes off to change his trousers on return to station.

Unfortunately we have seen more worrying behaviour by people at traffic incidents who are, because of the exploding cars they have seen on the screen, convinced they are doing the right thing.

There have been a number of times over the years where upon our attendance at a road traffic incident we have found the casualties laying outside of and away from the car, placed there by well meaning bystanders who fearing again that because the car was in an accident it was sure to explode. Then deciding the best thing to do was to drag out the injured and get them away from the vehicle. Such action can, and almost certainly has, caused further serious injuries to these casualties.

Should anyone come across an accident where people are injured inside a vehicle leave them in place! Lift up their head to clear the airway and hold their head steady, ideally from the back, with both hands to protect them from inflicting further damage to themselves by twisting and turning their neck. Reassure them and get someone to call the emergency services. This action with lots of reassurance, or tender loving care (TLC) as we know it, is very often all that is required. When the ambulance staff turn up tell them what you've done and stand aside to let the professionals do their work. This simple but effective quiet approach to a disaster can make a real difference between a victim recovering or not.

**Belt Up**

The law has required car drivers and front seat passengers to wear a seat belt since 1983 and considerable publicity has been given to the very positive reasons for doing this e.g. it will save your life! Despite this there remains a continuing fraction of the population who simply refuse to do it. The reasons they seem to have for this range from it's 'not cool' to 'just can't be bothered.' Whatever reason they have they always seemed very embarrassed, if they are fortunate enough to be able to talk, when they become our customers following their involvement in an RTA.

Probably the saddest no seat belt wearing incident we attended was one which resulted in little damage being sustained by the car and indeed little obvious damage to the 21 year old driver. Apart that is from a broken neck that killed him!

The accident occurred just after 06.00 hrs on a clear dry Saturday morning with little other traffic on the road. Judging by the marks on the central reservation and upon the road of the local dual carriageway where this occurred the car had been travelling at high speed when the young man lost control. The vehicle went into a spin of several rotations coming to a rest amongst some small trees. The driver himself had come to a rest sat upright in the front passenger seat after being flung from side to side in the vehicle. With no seat belt securing him the centrifugal forces took complete control of his body and dealt it a fatal blow. It was as we have seen only too often such a tragic waste of a young life in what was quite possibly a survivable accident.

Just a few weeks before I retired an opportunity presented itself which enabled me to personally question one of this feckless minority as we cut him from the wreck of his mate's car. Fortunately for him it had been a low speed crash and the vehicle came to rest amongst an entanglement of small trees. We treated him with great caution after he had quickly told us he had suffered neck injuries in a previous car crash!

Following an assessment it was decided to remove the tailgate of the car and back seat so as to enable a stretcher to be brought in through the rear. This was positioned so we could lay him carefully back on to it and firmly strap him down to remove him in a way which would mean the minimum movement of his neck. This is a common procedure used by the ambulance service and highly effective in completely immobilising the victim. Though as I pointed out to him that if we dropped him in the large water filled ditch, from which the snare of trees had saved the car from a watery end, to keep afloat he would have to swim by just blinking his eyelids!

As the team began their work I and another fire fighter physically held him to restrict his movements and administered a certain amount of TLC. Whilst doing this I became aware that his left leg was in a curious position pushed up against the left of the dashboard. It didn't appear too seriously injured but was certainly in a strange place. I asked him why it was there. "Oh" he said "I never wear a seat belt so I put my leg up on the dash to save me in case of an accident." Now to my mind on a 10 point scale of stupidity this was probably at 9.999! (10 being reserved for the man who used a lighter to see how much petrol remained in the tank of his motorcycle!) Here we had someone who had already survived one crash without a seat belt but suffered serious injuries as a result of it. To convince himself he was really stupid it seems he had tempted fate and lost once more! As he was suffering pain during his extraction from the vehicle I attempted to educate him that it was better to be 'uncool' and wear a belt than so cool you were dead cool!

# Chapter 10

## Severe Weather

Over the years there were several occasions when the consequences of severe weather presented us with quite different challenges from the fire and rescue incidents we attended.

### A Nasty Bout of Wind!

The Great Storm of 1987 when hurricane strength winds cut a swathe of destruction across the South of England caused a great deal of damage locally and we attended a number of calls to protect properties from trees which had or were in danger of toppling on to them. This was made all the more interesting by the added challenge of getting through roads blocked by trees which had fallen across them cutting Yateley off from the outside world for many hours. It was only by use of hand saws and brute strength that we managed to clear a path.

Downed power lines were a danger for us, and others, as we struggled to get through. These resulted in the loss of power to parts of our area for up to ten days. During this time we attended two house fires associated with this power loss, one from the careless use of candles and the other when a gas lamp was being replenished with a new canister and leaking gas ignited, both items being used to lighten the gloom

### The Shocking Effect of Lightning

Severe summer storms can wreak local havoc with lightning strikes and flooding from just a few minutes of torrential rain. Several incidents associated with lightning strikes have proved challenging and especially those which found us working in conditions where the storm still raged around us.

One afternoon we attended two consecutive calls which made us more than a little nervous of the elements and the highly charged electrical atmosphere we were working in.

The first call was to a mobile home which had sustained damage to its roof from the high winds commonly associated with these storms. As we arrived the storm seemed to have passed on and we quickly got to work tying down a salvage sheet over the damaged roof. But as we did so it seemed that the storm returned bringing with it dark heavy clouds which seemed to get lower and lower! As we stood upon the roof we could feel the power in the atmosphere. Quite literally our hair started to stand on end as it responded to the static electricity around us. Agreeing this was a hair raising experience we did not need we quickly descended and returned to the fire engine. Its four thick rubber tyres between us and the earth made us feel a whole lot safer.

We were not there long however before our control were on the radio. This time they sent us to a fire amongst bushes in a field adjacent to some gravel pits in the valley which makes up a large part of Yateley. It was teeming with rain by now and because of the wet conditions we were suspicious of the nature of such a fire. Attending we found our suspicions confirmed. Although smoke and flashes of flame were emerging from a bush in the middle of a field, it was not a simple fire. Laid in the bush was the broken end of a high voltage cable which normally hung between pylons across the field. A direct hit from a lightning strike had broken it and it was now sparking happily away in the wet conditions. We kept a healthy distance from it and radioed for the electricity board to come out.

As I waited for them I became concerned with the way the cable was sagging from the next pylon along. I walked over to this pylon and realised that the cable went over a gravel pit used as a fishing lake. In the centre of this lake about 60 metres from where I stood was a small island. It was a mound of about 10 metres in diameter with a large dead tree at its centre. On the island was a boat, a goat and a young woman. Why? I still have no idea!

Then appeared a young man from around some bushes near where I was standing. He said he was with the woman and had another boat on the bank of the lake. I explained to him my concerns that the sagging high voltage cable may fall into the lake. This could have fatal consequences for anything or anyone in it at the time.

Suddenly there was vivid flash of light and loud bang. I dived to the ground and sought out the safety of any stone or blade of grass I could hide behind. I looked up and saw a smouldering gash down the full length of the tree on the island. It had taken a direct hit from a bolt of lightning.

There was no sign of the young woman. Fearing the worst I grabbed the young man with the intention of commandeering his boat. We needed to get to the island as quickly as possible. Then the woman suddenly stood up from the position she had thrown herself, or been thrown by the blast. "I'm ok" she called across in a very shaky voice. Next she jumped into her boat and paddled over to us very quickly indeed. Incredibly she (and the goat) had been untouched by the lightning. She had only been a few feet away from the tree yet somehow had been spared a shocking fate.

We checked she really was ok then left them both with the suggestion that it was a good day to buy a lottery ticket as she would never have a luckier escape than that. I too hope never to be so close to lightning again. It had proved to be yet another trouser changing experience!

**Blasted Roof!**

Fortunately the next occasion we encountered the damage that this weather phenomenon can inflict it was several minutes after the strike.

In the middle of a hot summer's afternoon the skies over Yateley darkened to signal the approach of a storm. Soon the thunder was rolling out across the heavens. I had just returned to Yateley from my fulltime job in Reading and dropped into the station on the way home. I had decided to work on a backlog of the inevitable paper work. The volume of admin work had increased massively as the years progressed. As I opened the back door my pager warbled into life. Above its noise I could hear the chatter of the teleprinter detailing the address and type of the incident.

We were called to attend a fire in a roof following a lightning strike on a house just 100 metres from the station, although a row of trees masked this from view. Knowing the rest of the crew would be on their way I quickly put on my fire kit and grabbed a portable fire ground radio. I planned to walk over to the incident and assess the situation in preparation for the arrival of the pump. I told the next man in what I was doing and to listen to the fire ground radio in the pump as the crew kitted up and to get mobile as soon as possible. I then made my way through the trees. As I emerged the view before me was one of smoke and flame. A detached house had smoke pouring from its roof. The lightning had punched a hole through the tiles instantly setting fire to the timber joists and rafters. It had also damaged the water tank. This meant a twin threat to the house from both fire and flood!

My first concern was for the safety of anyone in the house at the time of the strike. It was with great relief to quickly learn from neighbours emerging from their own houses that the mother and baby who were in the property had both been downstairs and escaped unharmed. Although naturally they were quite shocked. I then heard one of the neighbours say "Thank goodness the fire brigade are here." I looked round expecting to see the fire engine but then I realised she meant me! So I felt obliged to get on and do something. The fire was well beyond my personal resources. It required an attack with hose and water from the pump. However it is often the small things one can do in a crisis which can make a difference.

118

The fire engine and crew were by now on their way but needed to travel about ¼ of a mile by road to get to me. Radioing them a situation report they were fully prepared for what confronted them. In the meantime I was able to close the mains water stopcock so as to stop more water being added to the problem and reduce the water damage by opening sink and bathroom taps to help drain the damaged water tank in the roof.

On arrival the firefighters were led by FF Mark West. It was an impressive sight as they burst out of the cab already rigged in BA. Grabbing a hose they were swiftly in the house and up the stairs attacking what had quickly developed into a severe fire. By now it had engulfed the whole roof space. I have a very clear vision from this time of Mark driving his stocky frame through the loft hatch to get at the flames, in this fighting mood the fire stood no chance and was quickly knocked down.

**The Flooding Merry-Go-Round**

Dealing with flooding incidents can seem straight forward i.e. we spend a lot of time at the scene, residents are happy to see us and thousands of litres of water are moved by our pumps. In truth however our presence can often be less effective than it may seem. Certainly we have performed many hours of salvage at such calls and a great deal of good work was been done in these times but often the problem of moving water is where to move it to!

There have been times when continuous severe weather in the form of days and days of heavy rain has drenched our area. Both the River Blackwater and the water table of the area itself have risen to levels which have caused severe, if isolated, flooding.

After one particularly heavy and extended period of rain the river became severely swollen and flooded so badly it seeped through an adjacent railway embankment and into a number of gardens and then houses which in turn backed on to this embankment. We were called and arrived to find people trying their best to bail the rising water out of their homes.

It was difficult to know quite where to begin so many were the houses affected but we set our pumps to work in the deepest water ensuring the results of our pumping went into the drains in the road at the front of the houses. In the meantime any spare crew members were busy cleaning out blocked up drains and helping the householders to salvage what they could.

We worked like this for several hours and it was during this time that hard working FF Bill Yarnall found a particular drain hidden from view in the filthy water which had had its metal cover removed. He found it in the most effective way by stepping into it. It was suggested that his waistline prevented him from dropping further down the hole. Wet but unbowed he continued his good work in his usual reliable way.

On we worked until a gentleman from Thames Water, who was the responsible water authority for the area, approached me. He explained that although lots of hard work and pumping was going on the drains into which we were pouring the water simply took this load and deposited back into the river a little way upstream of us. So effectively we were pumping the water round and round. I thanked him for this information and then asked him the best place for us to redirect this to. He shrugged and said there really wasn't anywhere as in that area all drains seemed to have common outlets i.e. into the river.

We had then the difficult task of leaving the residents to clear up the best they could as now understanding our pumping efforts were in vain we had to make ourselves available for other calls where we could be effective.

A similar occurrence, which reflected just how much rain had fallen, was when we were called to a 400 year old cottage in a low lying area of

Eversley. We arrived to find that the flooding they were suffering was actually coming up through the flag stoned floor of the property. The water table had risen to a point above the floor. There was no quick pumping out to be done as this flood would continue until the level of the water table fell again. We did what we could and advised the householder to hire a pump and operate it 24 hours a day until the water ceased to come in, which I understand is what they did. It was interesting to reflect that this flooding was the first record of it occurring in the 400 year history of the property.

The roads outside and the bar area inside the Royal Oak pub in Reading Road, Yateley have twice been affected by flooding following a severe summer storm. On both occasions an adjacent stream had burst its banks. The most memorable of these incidents was the first when prior to our attendance, and so unknown to us, someone had lifted the manhole covers in the flooded road in front of the public house. This was very murky and mucky water and impossible to see through. These facts probably accounted for the reason that FF Paul Atkinson managed as he waded through the flood to fall down one! Paul was the first to establish this tradition which, as explained earlier, it seems was maintained by FF Bill Yarnall. Paul quickly scrambled out and apart from a good soaking, which the rest of the crew agreed did him no harm, he was fine.

One of the problems we faced on these calls was again where to pump the water to and we had to go to great lengths to ensure that water we pumped away, into a road which subsequently went down to the River Blackwater, did not flood any other property on its journey to the river.

There was another reason for remembering so well the first call to the Royal Oak. It was at the expense of a particular senior fire officer of that time. When the deluge hit the area 4 fire engines from local stations were called to attend a number of separate incidents as Yateley seemed to be the target of the storm's wrath. With so many fire engines in use a senior officer was despatched to ensure all went well. As the work load for everyone subsided we coincidentally all found ourselves in the bar of the

Royal Oak, where the Yateley crew had spent quite a while in removing the water and subsequently assisting with the cleaning up.

The landlord was grateful and happily provided a free drink for all of the firefighters who had worked so hard that day. Now when the senior officer arrived, and being a man who enjoyed his drink, he thought this a good idea and agreed that as our work was complete we were no longer regarded as on duty so drinking was not a problem, except for the drivers of course. Indeed he so much enjoyed it that he insisted we had another round. So we did, and then hugely enjoyed the moment when the landlord upon pouring the last pint presented it to the officer together with a bill for the round. Arriving a little later than the rest of us he had not realised that there was only one free drink, but he did now!

**An Incredible Escape.**

In the winter of 2002 rainfall was high and over the Christmas period it continued to rain heavily. The River Blackwater was in full spate and had burst its banks in several places which resulted in numerous flooded fields, though fortunately no properties on this occasion.

At 20:47 hrs on New Years Eve we were called to assist our colleagues from Hartley Wintney at an incident which was reported as a car and people in the river just outside Eversley. As we drew near to the given destination we started to encounter flooded roads. Despite trying from several directions we had in the end to leave the pump at some distance from the scene and walk along flooded lanes too deep to drive through and then in turn across flooded fields. By the time we arrived the Hartley Wintney crew had found the victims, two men and a woman, all in their seventies, who were very fortunate indeed to have survived what must have been a very cold and shocking experience.

Their night had started well and they had been looking forward to an evening with friends playing cards and seeing the New Year in. The address they had been trying to locate was in a road at the end of which was a ford across the river. In normal conditions it is possible to negotiate this ancient crossing point but in the flood conditions of the night this quiet flowing river had become deep, swift and extremely dangerous.

Reaching the point on the road where it met the river they realised they had gone too far and attempted to turn around. This is where things went wrong. Their 4 x 4 vehicle was picked up by the strong current and floated off down stream into the darkness. Realising their predicament they acted quickly and forced their way out of the car into the water then remarkably managed to scramble up a bank and into a field.

This was as well as just a short distance from where they emerged their car became trapped under a low bridge where it became almost completely submerged. (See the photo which shows the vehicle the next day after the rain had stopped and the river had dropped several feet.) By now they were very wet and very cold. Fortunately one of the men had the strength to walk across the fields to the house which was their original destination and so raise the alarm.

With the roads so badly flooded the summoned ambulance could not get near the scene. So the fire crews, having wrapped the poor folks in blankets, carefully both carried and led them to the safety of the waiting ambulance which took them off to hospital for a full medical check up.

Although several hours were spent being checked over I understand that they all made a good recovery. It was a remarkable escape considering the dreadful conditions and the age of the victims. We were all very happy to return to our families in time to celebrate the passing of an old year which had finished in such a positive way.

Without doubt the most serious flooding we attended was as part of a relief operation in the village of Hambledon in the south of Hampshire during January 1994. The area had suffered considerable rainfall for some time and the geographical layout of the village surrounded as it was by hills was at the bottom of what could be described as a bowl. The water table, normally under the village, rose dramatically with the main road through it becoming a large stream of several inches in depth. Worse all of the cellars of the 19<sup>th</sup> and early 20<sup>th</sup> century buildings filled with water percolating into them through their floors and walls. The result was that there were very serious concerns about their foundations being washed away and much of the village destroyed. As a consequence of this many of the villagers reluctantly agreed to be evacuated.

Hampshire Fire Brigade was called at an early stage and commenced operations to pump the water away. It was though soon confronted with that common problem when dealing with floods just where to pump it to! The solution was that a series of pumps were used in conjunction with 12inch diameter hose laid along the street to pump the water from the top of the village through to the stream at the bottom of the village where it flowed naturally way.

The pumping operations ran for 24 hours a day and continued for more than a week until the water table receded. As a consequence this operation consumed large amounts of resource in terms of man hours and equipment. To satisfy this demand for manning crews were pulled in from all over Hampshire and firefighters from Yateley attended for 2 X 8 hour shifts.

I primarily remember this for the boredom of the occasion as all our duties consisted of were to ensure the pumps were kept fuelled and the water kept flowing through them. However several of the houses had very comfortable beds which for a few hours at a time served us well. It was a remarkable example of the power of water following repeated rainfall and of the success of the subsequent operation by the fire service which I am pleased to say achieved its goal of saving the village.

**All Hail!**

The summer storms in our area as in most others are very much hit and miss affairs in that on some occasions a location can remain bone dry whilst just a mile away severe flooding is encountered. This was certainly the case on one particular bizarre occasion when during a heat wave we dealt with a severe problem of icing!

We could clearly see the heavy dark clouds as they developed out of the remains of a hot sultry afternoon. But what wind there was pushed them north of Yateley away from our fire ground and into Berkshire. Then as the storm broke we could clearly hear the rumbling thunder and see the distant flashes of lightning.

It was not long before our pagers sounded and we found ourselves being sent in to help the fire crews in Berkshire who were becoming overwhelmed with calls to deal with flooding and lightning strikes. We were directed to a housing estate just south of Bracknell where the storm had appeared to centre itself.

Arriving we were confronted with a bizarre site of piles of ice scattered around the streets and, for some unfortunates, in the living rooms of their houses. The residents described what had happened.

The storm had broken above them. A massive fall of hailstones all about the size of a large pea cascaded down. They were so dense they covered the ground to over an inch in depth. Then torrential rain came flooding the area in minutes. As this floodwater ran off the drought hardened ground so it gathered up the hailstones which floated upon it. These in turn blocked drains greatly increasing the flooding which swept into the houses that had their doors open because of the earlier stifling heat. Here they formed piles of ice in living rooms and hallways. We did all we could to help them clear up and took part in the bizarre activity of shovelling these piles of ice out of the house and into dustbins. These were wheeled away outside and emptied into the road forming mini icebergs amongst the now receding floodwater where with the sun now returned they quickly melted.

# Chapter 11

## Community Safety

Responding to and dealing with emergencies in our community is certainly the key reason why we exist but this is by no means the only reason. We would actually prefer not to be called out if it means, as it so often does, that someone in our community is suffering. It is for this reason that we have spent so many hours over the years striving to educate people, most commonly children, to the dangers of fire and how these can be avoided.

Hundreds of children have visited the station to meet the firefighters and have a squirt with a hose reel. But not before they had also had clear and simple lessons on the importance of smoke alarms and what to do on discovering a fire.

In addition we have taken a regular and active part in the annual May Day Fayre, where we gave demonstrations on the consequences of Chip Pan fires and how we dealt with an RTA, including of course the importance of wearing a seat belt. We also regularly attended local fetes. In fact wherever we were we would always endeavour to provide advice which enhanced the safety of our community.

All of this work was performed completely voluntarily and so at no cost to the fire service. We did it because we cared. That's all.

In this book I have on several occasions been highly critical of the media but there should be no doubt that the local press, and Meridian Television news, contributed considerably to our safety messages. Their positive reporting of our fund raising and community safety work contributed directly to its success. I would in particular praise the writing of our local press reporter Sandra Marshall of the Camberley News & Mail and take this opportunity to publicly thank her for her advice and help over so many years.

## Target 2000

No book telling stories from the first 25 years of Yateley Firefighters would be complete without relating the one about our local community fire safety campaign. This campaign resulted in us raising over £33,400 and arranging the purchase and distribution of over 13,400 smoke detectors to children as a personal present for fitting into their bedrooms.

I will begin with the story of what was in my personal experience, the 'best' fire call I ever attended.

It was in the early hours of February 10th 2003 and we had received a call to a house fire in Yateley. As we pulled up outside the house I could see what appeared to be, and indeed was, a family group standing outside of the address. I was to discover this was the Jones family. I stepped down from the cab and the mother, Mrs Jones, approached with the memorable words "Thank God we had a smoke detector!"

A fire had developed in the integral garage of their house. A garage which contained two cars and all of the normal flammable substances found in any domestic garage from paint to aerosols to oil and petrol. The smoke travelled through the holes in the ceiling of the garage and up into the bedroom above where it activated the smoke alarm waking the family and enabling them to escape the fire and call us out.

Mr Jones then entered the garage and as the smoke gave such an early detection of the fire he was able to throw water over it and put out the flames, indeed all we did was to damp it down some more and remove the burnt material to the open. Just to be sure. There was no question that had the fire developed as it could, using the huge amount of fuel it had at its disposal, the family would have been extremely lucky to have survived the subsequent inferno. Indeed they would very possibly never have woken up! The detector which woke the family was one presented by us to the eldest daughter!

The reasons for us being able to do this started some 4 years earlier.

Though now difficult to comprehend prior to 1999 retained firefighters were positively discouraged from providing fire safety advice, no matter how simple the questions from our community may have been. Indeed I can clearly recall a senior officer of Hampshire Fire Brigade, in the 1980's, attempting to admonish me for suggesting that we should do this and being told by him that it was well beyond our capabilities! Total nonsense of course!

It is true that there is a substantial technical area to be addressed when advising on commercial or business premises and a great deal of training should be completed to become qualified to provide this. But the vast majority of questions we were being asked related to simple domestic issues. Issues such as what extinguisher was best to have in the home or the value of fire blankets in the kitchen. Later as smoke detectors became more affordable and readily available so questions on these and the best places to locate them in a home became more and more frequent and yet we were still, officially, not allowed to provide this, to us, common sense advice.

Slowly but surely as more and more fire officers retired and were replaced by new blood with more open minds, so things started to change. For us probably the most significant event was the appointment of a new Chief Fire Officer for Hampshire, Malcolm Eastwood. Now it was from the top down that pressure to change this type of thinking and replace it with a more open can do attitude began.

The change was, for the fire service, relatively quick and welcomed by all of us at Yateley. The shackles were thrown off by the commencement in 1999 of a community fire safety campaign promoted by Hampshire Fire & Rescue Service. This campaign focused upon firefighters providing a smoke detector for all school age children in their fire ground. Notably these were to be given freely as personal issue to each child with the instruction that they should be fitted in the child's bedroom. This was then and remains today a simple yet powerful idea.

I can clearly recall my reaction to this when I first heard it being explained during a fire safety lecture in late 1999. A lecture which we had anticipated would be just another presentation but one which, as it turned out, was probably the most significant we ever had and certainly the one which had the most impact!

From a personal perspective I was sold on this from the first moment. Indeed I recall how surprised I was at the time that the brigade had developed this and that here they were actively encouraging us to go out into our community and get involved. We did not require telling twice and I was hugely encouraged by the support for this idea from the rest of the station. We worked as a team in whatever we did and such support was important.

An underlying key driver for us to get involved was an incident which took place in 1995 when 5 children and an adult perished in a house fire in an adjoining fire ground to ours. This took place just a few miles from our station. The fire, it was discovered, started in a child's bedroom and no smoke detectors were fitted in the house. A few months after this and in our own fire ground just a few yards from the station, 6 children were taken to hospital suffering from smoke inhalation. One of them, smoking in bed, failed to extinguish his cigarette correctly. Only the baby's cries which woke the sleeping father prevented this from being a further horrific tragedy.

These events made me determined that we would do all we could to prevent fire deaths in our area and this scheme gave us the vehicle upon which to do it!

The campaign was a challenging one as the bottom line was that although encouragement and support was provided by the brigade there was no money! To achieve our goal we had to raise the funds for the purchase of the detectors, create and produce a presentation package for each child consisting of the smoke detector, instructions on its best location on the ceiling and regular testing plus a leaflet about the scheme itself. Finally we had to distribute them. All of our time involved with this was to be performed in a completely voluntary capacity. Despite all of this we saw no hurdles which could not be overcome and with some creative thinking in place we rose to the challenge, as in short it seemed simply to be the right thing to do. So we did it!

We solved each challenge piece by piece. With regard to fund raising we had over the years assisted many local organisations such as Yateley Lions and Sandhurst and Yateley Round Table with their own fund raising ventures. This involved taking the fire engine to the big local event of the year the May Day Fayre, to helping out clearing up after Bonfire night spectaculars to Carol singing. We approached these groups to return the favour.

Following presentations to them on the scheme we were overwhelmed by their support and generosity. As a community we are fortunate indeed to have such locally active and dedicated people in our midst and we always enjoyed working with them.

The packages we created ourselves with the help of a local supermarket who were persuaded to donate several thousands of their carrier bags to pack them in.

For the distribution we used the schools who, almost without exception, were delighted to help. We would take the detectors along bagged up to suit class numbers in redundant post office sacks. Then followed a presentation by us to the children where we told them of the special present we had for them. Then in full fire kit we explained just how each item of our kit protected us from fire so this smoke detector would protect them. The children, not to mention some of the teachers, love to see firefighters in uniform! At the end of the school day the teachers would distribute the packages to the class and ensure each child received theirs to take home.

These donations and help from the schools enabled us to provide a smoke detector for every child of school age in our fire ground by the end of 2001. In subsequent years we maintained this scheme, again following generous donations from a variety of groups including a grant from Yateley Town Council, ensuring that all reception class children continued to receive this potentially life saving gift.

We also promoted this scheme outside of our area and were delighted that some stations picked up on this and in turn set out to provide as many children as possible in their own fire grounds with a free personal issue detector for their bedroom ceilings.

It is true that there are some who, for their own reasons, are critical of the fact that not all detectors given away so freely will find their way on to the ceiling of the child's bedroom. This is correct but we believe, from subsequently talking to children whilst going about our business in the local area that the vast majority did. The scheme's value was well proven as confirmed by the Jones family incident, together with others where we have learned that these detectors have alerted people to a fire. Indeed in some instances the alert was so early that there was no need for them to call us as they were able themselves to stop a simple incident from escalating into anything more destructive.

The scheme was additionally strong in the fire safety message it gave, not just to the child but across the whole and often extended family. Also due to its voluntary nature and financed from charitable donations it was of no cost to the fire authority.

A proud moment came for us in 2005 when the scheme's value was recognised by its inclusion as a finalist in that year's National Community Fire Safety awards. An event a group of us from the station happily attended at the NEC in Birmingham. True we didn't win but we made certain that all of the most noteworthy players in the UK fire industry present knew of Yateley Fire Station and the very positive work we did.

It was then with this in mind we greeted with huge disappointment, not to mention some incredulity, the instruction from HFRS that after the spring of 2006 we were to stop this work as it was "No longer a part of their fire safety policy."

A new approach of providing a home fire safety check was put in place whereby a fire fighter would visit a home, perform a fire safety check and provide detectors where needed. Certainly a good idea and one for which firefighters would be paid to perform. But as a retained fire station Yateley were restricted by HFRS to carrying out just 6 of these visits per week and with over 10,000 households in the Yateley fire ground to cover this will take in excess of 33 years to complete! In the meantime many children will not have the protection provided to them by the original scheme.

Sometimes however management decisions such as this can result in other approaches being put into place which can in turn maintain and indeed expand the benefits of the original scheme, but away from the restrictive practices of those who tried to kill it.

All of us who have served at Yateley Fire station are proud of the fact that during our first twenty five years no one died in a fire on our fire ground and from the year 2000 onwards a significant reduction in house fires was experienced.

Some have said we have been lucky, and they are right, the harder we worked on our community fire safety the luckier our community became!

# Appendix

## History of Yateley & Hawley Fire Stations 1939 - 1945

In Britain the 1937 Air Raid Precautions Act set up, amongst other organisations, the Auxiliary Fire Service (AFS). Included in the Home Office war plans was an order placed through the Office of Works for emergency fire pumps. Eventually these were to number over 20,000 of twenty-five different types from fifteen manufacturers. As the first ones became available over the next two years they were issued to those local authorities whose AFS sections had been formed. Another part of the emergency legislation provided for fire brigades to co-operate on a regional basis for mutual support in the event of air attacks.

In March 1938 the Air Raid Precautions (Fire Schemes) Regulations were issued detailing what each fire authority had to include when submitting their schemes for an emergency fire service organisation. At this time, Rural District Councils were not designated as 'fire authorities' but they became so with the adoption of the Fire Brigades Act 1938 when it came into force in January 1939 with the requirement placed upon them to provide an efficient fire brigade in their area of jurisdiction. Prior to the Fire Brigade Act, there were 1193 separate fire brigades and after its introduction this number was increased to 1668.

Those who had decried the early AFS volunteers were soon forced to swallow their words as mounting casualties showed the fire services to be every bit as brave as front line soldiers.

Fire Brigades in 1939 were most commonly established and organised by the borough councils and little co-ordination of the services they provided existed until the threat of a second world war enable this to change. At the commencement of World War II the fire cover for Yateley was provided by the Wokingham Fire Brigade and that for Hawley, including Blackwater, was provided by Camberley Fire Brigade.

In 1939 Hartley Wintney Rural District Council commenced the setting up of fire stations in Yateley and Hawley under the command of the Auxiliary Fire Service (AFS), later to become the National Fire Service (NFS).

Little is known of the experiences of the brave souls who crewed these stations but it is understood that in the early days of their existence they attended the 'Blitz' suffered by several big cities.

There is anecdotal evidence of them fighting a large gorse and grass fire on the common near Blackbushe airfield, then known as RAF Hartford Bridge. An enemy aircraft seeing the fire decided to add his own bomb load to the conflagration. Without I am happy to say any injury to the firefighters working below. Additionally a number of aircraft operating into and out of the airfield crashed in local areas and it seems inconceivable that the Yateley and Hawley firefighters did not attend these.

The following is a description of the provision for fire cover, indications of how these stations were equipped, manned and some of the activities that took place during these war years.

Shown in normal text are extracts of the minutes of the Hartley Wintney Fire Brigade committee. Text shown in *italics* are press reports reproduced from archived issues of the Camberley News which quoted minutes of the Hartley Wintney Rural District Council and Yateley Parish Council meetings. These press reports are reproduced with the kind permission of the Camberley News.

Little news is given of the fire fighting work they undertook as such information would not have passed the censorship of those difficult times.

29th November 1938

First meeting of the newly formed Hartley Wintney Fire Brigade Committee. The committee was responsible for the fire stations in Hartley Wintney, Odiham and Crondall which together formed the Rural District Council Fire Brigade.

A letter was read from the Wokingham Fire Brigade stating that they were prepared to continue with existing arrangements to provide a fire service in the parish of Yateley. The committee clerk was instructed to ask what the cost would be for Wokingham to also provide an air raid precautions fire service (AFS) in Yateley.

With regard to the provision of a fire service in Hawley, a letter had been received from the Aldershot Fire Brigade stating that they were considering their position. The committee clerk was instructed to enquire with Hawley Parish Council to ascertain if they would prefer to be protected by the Aldershot Brigade or the Camberley Brigade.

26th January 1939

Wokingham had responded to the query (29 November 1938) stating that they may provide fire protection in Yateley, including AFS protection, for £35 per annum.

The Frimley and Camberley Urban District Council had written on 20 December to say that the possibility of them providing protection in Hawley would be considered at a meeting in February. In the meantime the Aldershot Brigade was to continue to provide the service.

9th February 1939

A letter from the Wokingham Fire Brigade asked whether a "squad of ARP workers" had been enrolled in the Parish of Yateley. It was pointed out that this matter must remain in abeyance pending the completion of the council's peace time scheme.

The Frimley and Camberley VDC had responded to confirm that they were prepared to offer fire protection in Hawley both in peace time and in time of war, subject to a payment formula being agreed.

12th April 1939
16 AFS firemen had been recruited for Hawley.

31st October 1939
A recommendation was accepted that 11 additional hydrants should be provided in the parishes of Yateley and Hawley to improve the fire protection in the area.

28th November 1939
Captain Cox of the Camberley Fire Brigade attended a meeting of the Fire Brigade Committee and explained affairs at Hawley.

The men recruited into the AFS had converted a car into a fire tender and it was suggested that the council contribute a sum of money for housing and maintaining the vehicle.

Following discussion it was decided that Camberley should, if considered necessary, provide a sub-station at Hawley and supply the necessary tenders, pump and associated equipment with all members of the AFS at that location to be under the control Captain Cox and that any costs considered necessary by the Camberley Fire Brigade be repaid by the Hartley Wintney Council.

It was reported that Mr F J Derbyshire of Japonica Cottage, Blackwater had been made a member of the Hawley AFS.

*23rd February 1940*
*Yateley Parish Council*
*Gorse Fires.*
*Miss C. M. Bischoff stated that a recent gorse fire came very near her garden. Replying, the Chairman stated that because the Parish Council had occasion to burn a certain patch of common, boys set fire to the*

*gorse. It was a dangerous practice and was discouraged. To prevent a possible serious fire he hoped boys would be more sensible, and not indulge in setting fire to the gorse. The meeting heartily concurred with the Chairman's sentiments.*

(I have included this report to demonstrate how little some things change. During my time at Yateley I too was regularly in hot dry weather making appeals in the local press about the problem of children lighting fires on the common.)

28th May 1940

At the request of the Hawley AFS, the chairman of the Fire Brigade Committee and Mr Weir visited their station on 27 May to discuss various matters. The Camberley Fire Brigade had loaned them a trailer pump which was towed by an old lorry. Mr J Jones of Blackwater had allowed a portion of his building to be used as a station for housing the vehicle and equipment. This building was actually situated in the Camberley area and it was considered advisable to rent a garage in the Hawley district if possible. A garage owned by Mr Kelsey in London Road was considered to be suitable for the purpose and it had been offered for £20 per annum. The lorry being used on a tender was very old and it had great difficulty. The committee recommended that enquiries be made for its replacement.

Members of the station were of the opinion that it would greatly assist them in many ways if some residents of Hawley would act as a liaison officer and it was suggested that Mr Fleming of Hawley undertake these duties.

The committee further recommended that a further 2 lengths of 75ft of hose be purchased for Hawley and that a messenger be engaged for calling members of the station to be paid of 10 shillings per annum.

*June 21st 1940*
*Hawley Fire Service.*

*Measures to improve the Hawley Auxiliary Fire Service were reported by the Fire Brigade Committee. There was a very keen group of men at Hawley, Mr. A. Ford Young said, but their equipment lacked many things, and most of all a suitable vehicle for the pump. That difficulty had been solved by the generous gift of an old 30 horse-power car. well suited to the purpose, by Mr. Fleming, of Hawley. The Fire Brigade was willing to fit it out themselves as a fire tender if the materials were provided, and Mr. Kelsey, of Hawley, had offered them a suitable garage at a rent of £12 per annum, which offer it was recommended should be accepted. The committee further recommended that two 75-feet lengths of hose be purchased for Hawley, and that a messenger be engaged for calling the members together for a fee of 10s. per annum.*

(The Hawley AFS Station was located on the A30 between Hawley Lane and Rosemary Lane, Blackwater. Originally on the western side of the road it then moved across to the eastern side. - Author)

*Yateley Fire Hydrants.*
*In response to a request from Mrs. V. Baillieu. of Much Common, Yateley, that a water hydrant be fixed at her own expense on or near her property, the committee recommended that a hydrant be fixed at a point to be decided on after inspection by Captain Woollcombe, the Chief Officer of the Hartley Wintney Fire Brigade.*

*Fire in the woods around caused by incendiary bombs was a real menace, but the local fire brigades had measures to deal with that eventuality.*

### HEATH FIRE
### ON HARTFORD BRIDGE FLATS
*Fanned by a strong breeze, a fire raged across the heathland of the Hartford Bridge Flats throughout Tuesday. The fire extended from the main road, halfway between Hawley road and the Ely Hotel to a short distance from the Cove-Minley road. It was first noticed at about 10:30am. About 100 yards in width for the first few hundred yards, the*

*fire spread quickly over a greatly increased width. Help was sent for and shortly lorry loads of soldiers arrived and fought the fire with shovels and beaters but it was not until late evening that they had beaten most of it out. Dense clouds of smoke issuing from it were seen by residents over a wide area.*

25th June 1940

It was reported that Mr Kelsey had agreed to allow his garage to be used to house the Hawley tender and pump. Mr Fleming had presented the Hawley unit a 34hp Minerva Saloon car which was being converted at a cost of £15.

*July 19th 1940*
*Yateley Fire Services.*
*When the question of providing a water hydrant at Much Common, Yateley, which Mrs. V. Baillie had requested might be fixed at her own expense, on or near her property, was raised at the meeting of the Hartley Wintney Rural Council on Friday, the Chairman of the Fire Brigade Committee, Mr. A Ford Young, stated that the Ministry of Home Security felt that the Wokingham Fire Brigade was not near enough to provide sufficient protection for that area. They had promised to provide a small trailer pump and equipment if an A.F.S. Group could be formed there. They would have to look out for someone to give them a car to which the trailer pump could be attached. Mr. Ford Young added.*

23rd July 1940

The chairman of the Fire Brigade Committee and the Chief Fire Officer had visited the Home Office and as a result the Home Office were prepared to provide a trailer pump and a range of equipment for Yateley Parish. This was considered to be a very satisfactory outcome as Yateley was not at that time covered by the Emergency Fire Brigade Organisation (AFS).

The Chief Fire Officer reported that he had been unable to find a motorist willing to loan or give a high-powered car for towing a tractor pump at Yateley and had therefore written to the Home Office for instructions as to how to secure a vehicle.

*August 16ᵗʰ 1940*
*Hawley Fire Service.*
*This display on Saturday began a gas mask and dry hose drill, by members of the A.F.S., on Hawley Green. A similar display was given minus the gas masks, at Sandy Lane: Hawley, after which the fire pump brought into action outside Hawley Church of England School. The chief purposes of the display were to let the villagers know they were being protected, and for them to be brought into contact those who were to protect them. After the display the A.F.S. members of the Hawley Parish Council including Mrs. E. J. Adams (chairman) and her husband, were entertained by Mr. R. A. D. Fleming. After a walk around the picturesque gardens of Hawley House tea was provided. After tea Mrs. E. J. Adams thanked Mr. Fleming, on behalf of the Parish Council for his gift, and for all he had done in connection with the fire service. Mrs. Adams also expressed the gratitude of the Parish Council to the men of the A.F.S., saying that in converting the motor car into a fire engine they had achieved something that most people considered impossible. The section, which has nine members, needs seven more, after which they will become a fully-fledged substation of the A.F.S. As a tribute to Mr. Fleming the fire engine was christened "Robert."*

27th August 1940
The AFS unit was now established at Yateley and training by the Chief Fire Officer had commenced. The Home Office issue equipment had arrived but the trailer pump was found to be damaged and it had to be returned for repair. A 1935, 31hp Buick had been purchased to tow the pump for £20. The Home Office had confirmed that they would fund the vehicle.

It was reported that a very successful display had been given by the Hawley AFS on 10 August on the cricket green at Blackwater after which the personnel and members of the Parish Council were entertained by the kindness of Mr and Mrs Fleming of Hawley Place.

(Note: Mr Fleming was recorded as being a 'transport officer'. Possibly a position held in the local ARP organisation. –Author)

A telephone had been purchased for Hawley fire station and a rest had been rented for 2/6d per week. A 300ft hose had been purchased for the station.

A fire had occurred in Blackwater. (No further details given - Author).

*September 16th 1940*
*The need for equipment for the local A.R.P. services was considered. A letter read in answer to one sent by the Council, from the Chief Executive Officer at Hartley Wintney, which stated that the Civil Defence Committee had decided to provide the A.F.S. with a trailer pump and equipment consisting of hose, ladders, etc. The A.F.S. party will be formed from the old Rescue Party, who have already begun to drill, under the leadership of Mr. G. C. Ives.*

(Mr G.C.Ives was at this time Clerk to Yateley Parish Council. He seemed to be very active in local affairs from being the first officer in charge of Yateley A.F.S. station to serving upon the committee of Yateley Cricket club. There is no family connection whatsoever between G.C.Ives and the author.)

24th September 1940
Yateley AFS asked to have a rest room for use during stand-to periods. Mr Fullbrook had offered his stables and part of his outbuildings free of charge to house the tender and trailer pump. However, as it was some distance from where most of the personnel were living, the offer was declined.

The station had received three calls, a plane crash on The Flats and two standbys at the station. It was noted that as Yateley had an AFS unit, the arrangement and agreements with Wokingham Fire Brigade could be terminated.

*September 27*<sup>th</sup> *1940*
*Auxiliary Fire Service.*
*Yateley has now its own A.F.S. section, which at the moment consists of nine members, who are being trained under the leadership of Mr. G. C. Ives. Equipment is expected to arrive soon, and when this happens more members will be required to make up the section to efficient strength. Men between the ages of 30 and 50 who are willing to give their services voluntarily, should apply to Mr. Ives, Vine Cottage, Cricket Hill, Yateley.*

24th October 1940
The Yateley AFS unit had again asked for a rest room. Mr Fulbrook had offered another location at his office for 2 shillings per week. It was a wooden building lined matchboard and fitted with a telephone.

Mr G Ives, the leader of the Yateley unit had been compelled to resign due to illness. A new leader has been appointed.

26th November 1940
The Home Office had issued a manual pump to Eversley Parish, Long Sutton, Hook and Crookham Ward (Crondall Parish).

*December 20*<sup>th</sup> *1940*
*Hartley Wintney RDC Meeting*
*Fire Brigade Matters.*
*It was reported that one manual pump with equipment had been issued to each of several parishes, including Crookham-street and Eversley.*
*The Council agreed to purchase 96 waterproof coats at a cost of 25s. each, subject to the consent of the Ministry of Home Security, for the personnel of the Fire Brigade.*

*Help from Camberley.*

*The Fire Brigade Committee, reporting that the Hawley Auxiliary Fire Service now had a pump and equipment, recommended that the agreement with the Camberley Urban Council for protection from fire of Hawley should be discontinued. Mrs. Adams protested that the equipment was not sufficient to cover the parish, especially as the new hydrants were not yet installed, and that it was rather unfair to sever that connection with Camberley, as the letter's Brigade had taken much trouble to train the Hawley A.F.S. Mr. A. J. R. Watts, the Controlling Officer, said that if necessary the Camberley Brigade would aid Hawley under the mutual assistance scheme, and the Council decided to refer the proposal back to the committee*

*December 27th 1940*
*A.R.P. and A.F.S.*
*Yateley has a well organized A.R.P Service and A.F.S., and those responsible have seen to it that these very necessary services are efficient. The A.R.P. system is functioning smoothly under the leadership of Major-General D. E. Cayley. About twelve men drawn from the previous Rescue Party have been trained by Mr. G. C. Ives (Clerk to the Parish Council). Necessary equipment, including a trailer pump and fire escapes have been provided by the Rural Council.*

28th January 1941
It was confirmed that volunteers had been found to operate the previously issued manual pumps in the following numbers:-

| | |
|---|---|
| Eversley | 7 men |
| Long Sutton | 5 men |
| Crookham Street | 7 men |
| South Warnborough | 6 men |
| Dogmersfield | 7 men |

*March 21st 1941*
*Hartley Wintney Rural District Council.*
*Payment to Firemen.*

*Reporting on discussions with the Home Office on the payment to firemen to recompense them for working time lost while standing by, the Fire Brigade Committee stated that rates to be paid to employers when standing by were to be fixed by the Regional Inspector. It was decided to rescind a resolution passed at the January meeting, authorizing payment at the rate of 1s. 3d. per hour, up to a daily maximum of 10s., in view of this awaited decision.*

*Yateley A.F.S.*
*The Fire Brigade Committee stated that the present premises occupied by the Yateley A.F.S. were inadequate and unsuitable, and recommended that premises belonging to a firm of brewers were more suitable. It was stated that the premises had been obtained without requisitioning.*

*On Friday a procession, consisting of members of the Home Guard, A.R.P. personnel, and members of the newly-formed A.F.S., under Mr. F. Powell, marched from the Drill Hall to the Green, where a display of hose drill was given by the A.F.S., and this was much appreciated by all present. Mr. A. E. T. Gibbs, Chairman of the Parish Council, gave a short speech.*

25th February 1941
It was reported that the premises at Yateley were unsuitable and it was suggested that the premises owned by Messrs May and Co, Brewers, Basingstoke and let to Mr Watts would fit the needs. At the time it was suggested that it may be possible to secure these premises by a requisition order.

1st April 1941
The premises owned by Messrs May and Co had been acquired on mutual terms

The Fire Brigade Committee gave consideration to the fact that the brigade and its Auxiliary Fire Service units were not organised directly in line with the Emergency Fire Service organisation scheme as laid down by the Government in the 1937 ARP Act.

It was decided that the 3 stations incorporated into the Brigade would henceforth be known as 'sections' each with a 'Captain' in charge and each having a 'Second Officer' to deputise for the Captain.

The Auxiliary Fire Service units would be organised as laid down by the Government and would consist of a Commandant in charge, Deputy Commandant, Patrol Loaders, Leading Firemen and AFS Firemen.

Mr W L Waide was appointed Commandant with Mr Fooks as Deputy. Each section of the AFS, namely at Hartley Wintney, Odiham, Crondall, Hawley and Yateley would have a Patrol Leader in charge responsible for the general activities of the AFS in support of the regular fire brigade and its captains.

Each AFS unit would consist of three crews of five. Each crew would have a Leading Fireman working in support of the Patrol Leader. It was agreed that the AFS officers would be elected by 'popular ballot' at local level.

It was hoped that the changes would unify the position throughout the District and assist the smooth running of the general organisation.

AFS units attached to the Regular Fire Brigade stations at Hartley Wintney, Odiham and Crondall were advised that their designated Patrol Officer would work in consideration with the Captain at that location who would be regarded as the senior officer.

*April 4*[th] *1941*
*A.F.S. Dance.*
*A dance for members of the Yateley A.F.S. and their friends was held in the Drill Hall, Yateley, on Wednesday, and over 200 local people spent a pleasant evening dancing to the music of the Rhythm Swing Band, of*

*Fleet. Many men in H.M. Forces were present. Mr. A. E. Fidler performed the duties of M.C., while Mr. F. Powell leader of the Yateley A.F.S. and members of the A.F.S. acted as stewards. Refreshments were provided by Mr Hopper. The winners of the spot dances were: 1. Miss Powell and Pte Barber; 2, Miss Fletcher and Pte.Mayes; 3, Miss McLean and Pte. Bostrom. The holders of the lucky tickets were Miss Fullbrooks and Staff-Sergt Bellamy.*

*April 18<sup>th</sup> 1941*
*A.F.S. Training.*
*Nine members of the Yateley Auxiliary Fire Service are to be paid the training fee of £1 each after completing 30 hours' training. This was approved at a meeting of the Hartley Wintney Rural Council on Friday, when it was stated that the men concerned are Messrs. F. C. Powell, F. C.Bird, C. Skeats, W. Harrison, L. Head, H. Aldridge, H. J. Powell, J. W. Mitchell and C. E. Wheeler.*

*Similar fees have been earned by the following members of Hawley A.F.S: Messrs. F. Hough, C. C. Tice, J. Rone, K. E. Poulter, C. E. Butcher, R. E. Chett and W. Watts.*

22nd April 1941
It was reported that the premises conversion at Yateley was almost complete.

*May 16<sup>th</sup> 1941*
*A.F.S. Enrolments.*
*Applications for enrolment m the Auxiliary Fire Service were approved by the Hartley Wintney Rural Council at a meeting on Friday. The applicants included.*
*R. S Coombes. of 2, Herdcote. Cricket-hill.*
*W. G. T. Neville. of 3, Council Houses. Vigo-lane. Yateley.*
*E. J. Brooker, of Heathcote, Wellington-road. Sandhurst.*
*It was stated that satisfactory medical reports had been received in each case.*

*The thanks of the Council were extended to members of Yateley Auxiliary Fire Service for their work in adapting the fire station at Yateley which was stated to be practically completed. Recommending the Council to take this course the Fire Brigades Committee said the work of the A.F.S had resulted in an appreciable saving.*

27th May 1941
A rest room for Hawley had been secured in a room over a garage opposite the fire station housing the tender and trailer pump.

(Barely had the new organisation structure been initiated when the Government decided to bring together all Local Authority fire brigades under the banner of the National Fire Service (NFS). This took place on 18th August 1941. – Author)

Under the newly formed NFS, the country was divided into 'Fire Forces' and each Fire Force was divided into Divisions and Sub-Divisions. A standard method of identifying stations and vehicles attached to stations was adopted.

Yateley and Hawley became part of No 14 Fire Force, situated in Sub-Division 1 of Division 'A'. Yateley was designated station 'S' and Hawley was designated station 'T'. The full designation for each being:
- Yateley: 14A1S
- Hawley: 14A1T

(In 2006 the station designation of Yateley Fire Station in the Hampshire Fire & Rescue Service structure is 14. A curious coincidence. - Author)

*September 19<sup>th</sup> 1941*
*Hartley Wintney Rural Council*
*Crop protection*

*The Fire Brigades Committee stated that volunteer fire crews were standing by every night and added that an additional pump and two mobile dams had been received.*

*Referring to the reorganisation of the country's fire services into a national fire force the Chairman said the Fire Brigades Committee had now ceased to exist.*

*December 19$^{th}$ 1941*
*Fatal Road Accident - Charles Wheeler 4 Knellers Cottages, lorry driver's mate - killed at Bagshot while examining rear light. Obituary: Charles Edward Wheeler (31) of 4 Knellers Cottages*

*Yateley folk will have read with regret the report in our last issue of the tragic death in a road accident at Bagshot, of Mr. Charles Edward Wheeler, of 4, Knellers Cottages, at the early age of 31. Mr Wheeler was born at Eversley and attended school there, and for the past few years has been working as a driver for a Yateley firm. He was a keen member of the A.F.S. at Yateley, and his popularity with local firemen can be realised from the fact that twenty-four fire brigades were represented at his funeral. Mr Wheeler's father was killed in the Battle of the Falkland Islands in 1914, and by some strange coincidence he, too, was 31 years old. The funeral took place at Yateley Parish Church on Wednesday, and was conducted by the vicar. the Rev. R. F. Pechey. The coffin was borne by Firemen Harrison. Skeets. Coombs, Yeomans, Aldridge and Brooker of the Yateley A.F.S., and Mr.G C. Ives also represented the Yateley squad. Among the twenty-four fire brigades represented were those from Fleet, Hartley Wintney, Odiham and Aldershot and a wreath was sent from the combined local brigades and one from the Yateley A.F.S. A wreath was also sent from the children of Hartley Row School, whom Mr. Wheeler used to drive to school from Yateley every morning in the course of his work.*

*April 10<sup>th</sup> 1942*

*A.F.S. Dance*

*A very happy evening was spent by about two hundred people in the Drill hall on Easter Monday when a dance was organised by the Yateley Fire Service. Music was provided by Joe's band and a substantial sum was raised for providing comforts for the men of the Yateley Fire Service.* (Dances were very popular at the Drill hall on a Wednesday night during the war and there are references to a fair number being run by the firefighters. Though not usually for their own comforts! The Drill Hall was located on the Reading Road in Yateley where the shops known as 'The Parade' are today. It suffered the indignity of catching fire and burning down in 1957.)

*October 30<sup>th</sup> 1942*

*Fire broke out in the dining room of "Harpton Lodge," Yateley, the residence of Mrs. Majendie, on Tuesday. While help was being summoned members of the household ripped up the floorboards and subdued the outbreak by the use of fire extinguishers. This prompt action prevented the fire spreading, and the damage was not extensive.*

*January 15<sup>th</sup> 1943*

*N.F.S. DANCE.*

*Wednesday's dance at the Legion Hall, Yateley, was arranged by the National Fire Service, and was much enjoyed by a large company. Music was supplied by Ralph and his boys.*

*August 6<sup>th</sup> 1943*

*Yateley Village Green on Bank Holiday Monday was crowded with people who enjoyed the fete arranged for them by the Yateley and Hawley Branch of the British Legion. The outstanding event was a tug-of-war between the Yateley Firefighters and a Royal Air Force team which resulted in a win for the firefighters.* (Although we did not know it at the time the tradition of Yateley firefighters participating in such events was rekindled in the early 1980's when on three occasions in succession we won the "It's a Knockout" competition. Held as part of the May Day Fayre every year on Yateley Green. - Author)

*August 27<sup>th</sup> 1943*
*FIRE AT BLACKWATER*
*AN APPRECIATION.*
*Mr. W. Comley, of The Fairfleld, Frogmore, Blackwater, writes:*
*"I am an amusement caterer, and for the past fortnight I have had my equipment on a piece of ground in Minley Road, Cove. At about 2.15 a.m. on Sunday I was awakened by shouts of "Fire!" Looking out of my caravan window I saw that one of my lorries was burning furiously. There was great danger of the whole of my equipment being burned out. The fire service had been called out, and quite a number of local residents arrived with stirrup pumps, and between them the fire was got under control. Had it not been for the untiring efforts of the local inhabitants the whole of my equipment would have been destroyed. I beg to tender to all those who rendered such unselfish and untiring assistance my most sincere thanks and gratitude for their magnificent efforts. Without their help and timely warning I should have lost my all. I say to all the local inhabitants, 'Thank you.'" I most respectfully suggest to the Chief of the Fire Services that he would be rendering a very great service to the public if his men were instructed as to the position of the hydrants. Had the fire been confined to residences it may have been more serious than it was, there may have been loss of life through the lack of knowledge where to look for the hydrants. That state of affairs should not exist in the public service."*

In December 1944 the establishment at Yateley and Hawley were recorded as:

Yateley:
- 3 Leading Firemen
- 15 Firemen
- 3 Firewomen

Hawley:

- 1 Leading Fireman
- 4 Firemen
- 1 Leading Firewoman
- 5 Firewomen
- 1 Light trailer pump

*August 11th 1944*
*A Good Job.*
*A pond which has been a constant nuisance to the patients and staff of the Yateley Hospital has now been cleaned and drained. The matter has been under consideration for some time and recently Colonel Bannaiyne, in consultation with the District Engineer, obtained the co-operation of the N.F.S. who pumped the pond dry and cleared out the drainage pipe.*

*November 24th 1944*
*Since then further Council meetings have been held, when the Fire and Ambulance services have been reviewed, and the attention of the Rural Council drawn to some of the weaknesses in these services. It was disclosed, in the review of fire precautions, that the Camberley N.F.S. will be responsible for dealing with outbreaks of fire in Yateley.*

Yateley and Hawley NFS Firefighters were finally stood down and the stations closed in the summer of 1945.

# Additional Memories Yateley Fire Station 1939 - 1945

Additional memories from Benji Wilmer and Marjorie Lovell:

Yateley's first fire engine from 1941 to early 1943 was an open top Buick saloon (large car) with a cradle built on top to carry the ladders. It is believed to have been donated for this purpose by a local person but no record exists as to just who this was.

It towed the large Scammel pump supplied by the War Department. This first engine was replaced in early 1943-1945 with a closed in van type appliance again supplied by the War department.

The fire station was located on what is now the car park of the White Lion public house in Reading Road. Nothing remains of this building but the large tree still in existence outside the pub and on the corner of Reading Road and Village Way was used by those firefighters to hang hose upon to dry.

Regular hose training took place at local sites such as Eversley Water Mill, Yateley Green pond, Cricket Hill pond (now called Wyndams) and several standpipe locations the number of which had improved considerably from beginning of the century. Water pressure at that time was from any standpipe 200lb/sq inch.

The crews were all men, women not being allowed to undertake such duties at that time. However women were used in an important communications role and staffed the telephones.

When they were needed crews were summoned to the station by a siren or the 4 crews undertook in turn 12 hour night duties 7pm to 7am. Unless the siren had gone. For these night duties they were each paid 3 shillings a night or a supper!

In the later years of the war some of the personnel serving at the station were as follows.

Leading Firemen.              Richard 'Dicky' Bird
                                  Albert Fiddler
                                  Bill Harrison
                                  Ted Brooker

One crew:

Leading Firemen.              Richard 'Dicky' Bird
                                  Dick Yeomans
                                  Edwin Chandler
                                  Buck Lee
                                  Lou Head
                                  Johnny Mitchell
                                  Benjy Wilmer

Telephonist – Mrs Bird

Other crew members.        Charlie Skeets
                                  Dennis Skeets
                                  Ted Harris
                                  Ted or Bob Coombs

Telephonist – Olga Stretton
Telephonist – Marjory

## **Additional Memories Hawley Fire Station 1939 - 45**

Additional memories from Mrs Hough of New Road Blackwater:

In 1941 Mr Carey-Barnard of The Elms, Blackwater collected names of men interested in forming an Auxiliary Fire Service. These men then received fire fighting tuition at Camberley Fire Station in The Avenue, including Captain Cox & Tom Cattermole. Mr Robert Fleming of Hawley House gave them the chassis of a car (Italian make). The men renovated it in Joseph 'Joby' James, a well known local garage owner, yard on the Hampshire side of Blackwater bridge into a fire engine. It towed a Scammal pump – provided by the War Department via Hartley

Wintney District Council, which also supplied Welligton boots, overalls and tin hats. On the engine was a ladder – hosepipes, stirrup-pump and a stand pipe. This fire engine was named Robert after Mr Robert Fleming.

The first station was 'housed' in the garage of Rose Hill in the London Road, the residence of Mr & Mrs Kelsey. This property no longer stands but was on the western side of the London Road approximately halfway between Hawley Lane and the bridge over the River Blackwater. When the sirens sounded the men made their way there – there was a telephone in the garage.

In later years the station moved to the opposite side of the road in the stables at a property called The Wilderness which again is no longer standing.

Following the decision in 1941 to establish the National Fire Service, some men were called up into the whole time fire service and Fred Hough and Reg Poulter were sent to Southampton and remained there for the duration of the war.

Acknowledgements and thanks for information relating to this Appendix:
Yateley Society
The Wartime Fire Services in Britain. By B S Baxter
Deputy Chief Officer Alan House, Hampshire Fire & Rescue Service
Marjory Lovell
Benji Wilmer
The kind permission of the Camberley News.

# YATELEY FIREFIGHTERS

## 1980 – 2006

| | |
|---|---|
| SUB.O. COLIN IVE | 1980 – 2006 |
| LFF. PAUL CULLEN | 1980 –1991 |
| LFF. JOHN HICKS | 1980 – 2004 |
| LFF. DANNY RANDALL | 1980 – |
| LFF. CHRIS SAYERS | 1986 – 1999, 2001 – |
| LFF. CLIFF TARRANT | 2006 – |
| FF. JOHN ASHBY | 1980 – 1983 |
| FF. PAUL ATKINSON | 1980 – 1984 |
| FF. MICK BARTON | 1990 – 2000 |
| FF. RICHARD BENTO | 1999 - 1999 |
| FF. JOHN BENTLEY | 1982 – 1985 |
| FF. MARTIN BONE | 1983 –1999 |
| FF. KIM BLUNT | 2004 – |
| FF. DARREN BUCKLAND | 1995 - 2005 |
| FF. STEVE CAPP | 2002 - |
| FF. CHRIS COLE | 1985 - 1995 |
| FF. PHIL COOK | 1985 - 2005 |
| FF. JOHN CHIVERS | 1980 – 1991 |
| FF. JOHN DEAN | 1980 – 2000 |
| FF. MARK DODDS | 1987 – 1989 |
| FF. MICK ELLIS | 1990 – 1997 |
| FF. IAN FRY | 1997 – 2000 |
| FF. ALAN FULCHER | 1983 – 1985, 1986 – 1987 |
| FF. DAVID GARWOOD | 2003 – |
| FF. STEVEN GEEN | 2001 - |
| FF. NORMAN GIBSON | 1984 –1997 |
| FF. DEREK GRIFFITHS | 1991 – 1999 |
| FF. CLAYTON GROVES | 2003 – |

| | |
|---|---|
| FF. MICK HARTNETT | 1995 - 1995 |
| FF. GARY HYDE | 1998 - |
| SC. DAVE NEWMAN | 1980 – |
| FF. CHRIS PARKER | 1992 – 1999 |
| FF. RYAN PRATLEY | 2001 - |
| FF. CHRIS RIX | 1980 – 1983 |
| FF. BILL ROBBINS | 1980 – 1998 |
| FF. ANTONY RUSSELL | 2006 – |
| FF. IAN STONES | 1999 - 2005 |
| FF. STEVE THOMSON | 1982 – 2004 |
| FF. JOHN WALLACE | 1986 – 1988 |
| FF. MARK WEST | 1980 – 2003 |
| FF. DUNCAN WEST | 1986 – 1987 |
| FF. ANTONY WHITE | 1999 - |
| FF. NIGEL WHITE | 1999 - |
| FF. BILL YARNALL | 1998 - |
| FF. PETER YOUNG | 1989 - 1990 |